Contents

ACKNOWLEDGEMENTS

The project team would like to thank the headteachers and teachers who kindly agreed to take part in the research, either by completing our questionnaires and/or participating in interviews.

Thanks are also due to all the NFER staff who were involved in the production and publication of the report, particularly Sunita Bhabra for carrying out interviews; Barbara Lee for directing the project and commenting on the report; Rachel Felgate for the analysis of survey data; Wendy Keys who wrote the research proposal; and Alison Bannerman for providing administrative support to the project. Thanks also to Peter Earley and Neil Ferguson of the Institute of Education, London, for their comments on the draft questionnaires and final report.

This project was commissioned by the National Union of Teachers and jointly funded by them and NFER.

Chapter 1

The Research Project

1.1 Introduction

Since its introduction in 1992, the Office for Standards in Education (OFSTED) system of inspection has provoked intense interest and debate regarding its effects on schools. This debate has focused on whether the OFSTED system is fulfilling its aim of 'improvement through inspection', and at what cost to teachers, schools and LEAs. Over the last nine months, the publication of several reports and the House of Commons Select Committee enquiry on the work of OFSTED have attracted considerable media attention and again raised the public profile of school inspections.

By the end of 1998, all primary and secondary schools in England had been inspected at least once. A relatively small proportion of these were judged to be failing to provide an adequate standard of education and were subsequently placed on the special measures register.[1]

In 1998 the National Foundation for Educational Research (NFER) was commissioned by the National Union of Teachers (NUT) to undertake a research project on these 'failing' schools. It was felt that although a substantial amount of research had been carried out on the conduct and effects of inspection, a comparatively small proportion of this research had been specifically targeted at special measures schools. In addition, most of the research on special measures has been based on case studies of a small number of schools. The current research project aimed to redress this imbalance by conducting a survey of all schools which were at that time (or had previously been) on special measures. The specific aims of the research were to look at the effects of inspection and special measures on different aspects of school life, including:

---

[1] 719 schools had been placed under special measures by the time this research project started. This figure is based on information supplied by OFSTED.

- school monitoring;
- teachers' workload, health and stress levels;
- professional support and relationships between staff, the LEA, the governing body and parents;
- school improvement;
- staff morale;
- staffing (including staff turnover, retirements, recruitment).

In addition, the project looked at initial reactions to the outcome of inspection and at the experiences of schools which have been removed from the special measures register.

1.2 Methodology

The research was carried out by means of:

- Survey 1: a questionnaire survey to schools on the special measures register and a matched sample of schools which had never been on special measures.

- Survey 2: a questionnaire survey to schools that had been removed from the special measures register.

- Interviews with headteachers and teachers at 18 schools which were then (or had previously been) on special measures.

Originally the project team had hoped to contact all schools which were placed on special measures between 1993 and 1998. However, following consultation with the LEAs concerned, 44 of these special measures schools were excluded.[2] The LEAs in question advised us that it would not be possible (due to school closure) or advisable (e.g. due to high staff turnover or school reorganisation) to contact these schools.

---

[2] In accordance with NFER policy, LEAs were informed of the research before schools in their areas were contacted.

1.2.1 Survey 1

There were two samples in Survey 1. Sample A was made up of 451 schools which were on the special measures register in 1998 (see Table 1.1). Information on these schools was obtained from OFSTED. In the period between receiving this list from OFSTED and the actual return of questionnaires in April/May 1999, some of the schools had been removed from the register. (One-quarter of the headteachers and 26 per cent of the teachers who returned questionnaires said that their schools had recently been removed from special measures.) Their responses were analysed with the rest of the Sample A questionnaires in Survey 1.[3] This did not pose any real problems for the project methodology as the questionnaires were designed to accommodate schools which might have recently come off special measures.

A matched sample (B) of 482 schools which had never been on special measures was drawn from the Register of Schools, an annually updated database of all schools in England and Wales held by the NFER. The latter group were included in order to investigate how the experience of 'failing' schools differs from that of other schools. The two samples were matched in terms of the socio-economic background of pupils (based on the proportion eligible for free school meals), year of inspection and type of school.

Table 1.1: Number of schools to whom questionnaires were sent (Survey 1)

School type	Sample A: special measures schools	Sample B: schools which had never been on special measures
Primary	311	325
Secondary	83	91
Special	57	66
Total	451	482

Self-completion questionnaires were developed for teachers and headteachers. Most questions were common to both, though the headteachers' questionnaire was more

---

[3] These questionnaires were not analysed with the Survey 2 cohort (schools which had been released from special measures) as the two groups were asked different questions.

detailed and asked for information on staffing, pupil numbers and the key issues for action identified by the OFSTED inspection team.

Since the objective of the research was to compare the experience of the two types of schools, headteachers at special measures and non-special measures schools were sent identical questionnaires, as were teachers in both samples. However, an additional section was included for completion by respondents at special measures schools only.

Questionnaires were designed so that staff could complete most sections, regardless of whether they had been in the school for the OFSTED inspection. The aim of the project was to look primarily at what happened **after** inspection, rather than at the preparation and inspection week itself. A small proportion of the overall sample had had their inspection before January 1996 (see Appendix 1 for dates of inspection). Because of the amount of time which had elapsed, these schools were not asked questions relating to the period before or immediately after the OFSTED inspection. It was felt that even teachers who had been there for the inspection might not be able to remember factual information, such as the amount of sick leave they had taken during this period.

The draft questionnaires were piloted in March 1999. Replies were received from a total of 34 heads, deputy heads and teachers, and the questionnaires were redrafted in light of their comments. The names of those contacted for the pilot study were provided by the NUT.

The survey was administered in April 1999. A questionnaire was sent to all headteachers and either two teachers (in the case of primary and special schools) or four teachers (in secondary schools). All questionnaires were sent to the head who was asked to complete his/her own copy and to distribute the rest to a sample of teachers, using criteria set by the NFER.[4]

---

[4] Headteachers were asked to pass on questionnaires to teachers whose names appeared first and last on the school staffing list.

Two reminder letters were sent to schools: one at the end of April, the other during May. In both cases, the letters were sent to headteachers who were asked (where appropriate) to return their own questionnaires and to remind teachers to do the same.

1.2.2 Survey 2

Survey 2 was smaller in scale, consisting of 196 schools which had been removed from the special measures register (see Table 1.2). The survey was administered in exactly the same way and at the same time as Survey 1. The questionnaires were sent to headteachers and either two or four teachers (depending on phase of schooling). Questionnaires were distributed by the headteacher, and two reminder letters were sent.

Table 1.2: **Number of schools to whom questionnaires were sent (Survey 2)**

| | *School type* | | | |
	Primary	*Secondary*	*Special*	*All schools*
Number of questionnaires	134	33	29	196

1.3 Response rates for Surveys 1 and 2

The number of questionnaires sent and response rates for Surveys 1 and 2 are shown in Table 1.3 and Table 1.4 below.

Table 1.3: **Number of questionnaires sent and response rates (Survey 1)**

	Number of questionnaires sent	*Number returned*	*Response rate %*
Heads	933	425	46
Teachers	2,214	737	33
Total	3,147	1,162	37

Chapter 2

After Inspection –
Schools' Responses

2.1 Introduction: the OFSTED inspection process

The inspection of secondary schools by OFSTED inspectors started in 1993 and was introduced into primary and special schools a year later. These Section 10 (formerly Section 9) inspections are normally conducted by teams of independent inspectors who are registered with and under contract to OFSTED. Some are undertaken by Her Majesty's Inspectors (HMI) and Additional Inspectors (OFSTED, 1999).

OFSTED inspectors must report on a number of matters, including: the quality of education provided by schools; educational standards; the spiritual, moral, social and cultural development of pupils; and the efficient management of financial and other resources. These matters are judged on the basis of observations during the inspection and also by consulting documents provided by the school. OFSTED provides the inspectors with information about the schools' results in national tests, which allows them to make comparisons with local and national standards (Ferguson *et al.*, 1999a).

If the judgement is made that a school is failing or likely to fail to provide an acceptable standard of education, and Her Majesty's Chief Inspector (HMCI) agrees, then the school is made subject to special measures.

This chapter looks at how respondents in the current project viewed the outcome of the inspection and their initial reactions. Data are derived from Survey 1 and the interviews.

2.2 Inspectors' judgement of the school

Respondents were asked whether, in retrospect, the OFSTED inspectors' judgement had been a fair reflection of the quality of education in the school at that time. Nearly three-quarters of heads and teachers at non-special measures schools said that the judgement was fair (Table 2.1). However, only one-half of headteachers and less than one-third of teachers at special measures schools agreed with the outcome, whilst most of the others said that it was too negative/much too negative.

Table 2.1:   Inspectors' judgement of the school

	Schools on special measures		Schools not on special measures	
	Heads	*Teachers*	*Heads*	*Teachers*
	%	%	%	%
Much too positive	1	0	0	0
Too positive	2	2	6	3
A fair reflection	51	30	72	70
Too negative	20	32	15	20
Much too negative	10	24	5	3
Unable to say	6	3	2	2
No response	10	9	2	3
N	173	294	255	442

Because percentages are rounded to the nearest integer, they may not sum to 100 in all cases.

Interestingly, a small percentage of respondents from special measures schools indicated that the outcome was too positive. This was because the schools in question did not 'fail' their OFSTED inspections: they were put on the special measures register later on, presumably by HMI. This may explain why, in retrospect, their OFSTED inspection seemed too positive.

One of the overall findings of the research has been that headteachers are consistently more positive about inspection, compared with teaching staff. This is particularly evident in the response to this question – the percentage of special measures heads who thought the outcome was fair is considerably higher than that for teachers. One possible reason for headteachers more positive view on the outcome of inspection is that nearly one-half of this group joined **after** the school was placed under special measures. There was a statistically significant link between headteachers' views on the outcome of inspection and whether they themselves worked in the school at the time of the inspection. Headteachers who joined after the inspection were more likely to say that the outcome was fair. Recent research also suggests that headteachers who regard themselves as 'new' do not feel as 'threatened by inspection as established heads and are more open to its possibilities' (Ferguson et al., 1999b).

Interestingly, the level of agreement between heads and teachers was noticeably higher at schools which were not on special measures.

2.3 Initial reactions to the outcome of inspection

Previous research suggests that the period after inspection can be quite traumatic in schools which have been placed on special measures. The situation has been compared to a bereavement:

> People's reactions to traumatic events such as a death in the family are said to go through a number of stages. Inspection appears to be no different and the acronym SARAH usually describes the process experienced by most schools and governing bodies. It refers to the stages of: shock; anger; rejection; acceptance; help (Earley, 1997).

In the current research, heads and teachers who were working in the school at the time of the inspection were asked to describe their initial reaction to the outcome. Not surprisingly, there were considerable differences between the special measures and non-special measures cohorts. The reactions at SM schools were similar to those described above, with respondents initially finding it difficult to believe what had happened and many rejecting the findings as inaccurate/unfair. The main points made by respondents at **special measures schools** are summarised below.

a) The inspection was flawed.

Just over 40 per cent of teachers and one-quarter of headteachers at special measures schools said that the inspection was flawed in some way and/or the outcome was unfair. Respondents who provided further detail focused on the team's failure to take into consideration the particular circumstances of the school. For example, the school was pre-judged; the socio-economic background of school was ignored; the inspectors focused too much on some things (or people) and not enough on others; the inspectors only saw part of the evidence and the school's strengths were overlooked. Respondents made comments such as 'The inspectors took no account of the school's circumstances'. Other problems identified by respondents seemed to be inherent to the system of inspection itself, rather than a failing of a particular OFSTED team; for example, a one-week inspection every four years does not give a realistic view of the school.

A related point made by about one-tenth of teachers was that members of the inspection team were not adequately qualified or experienced; or they did not behave in a professional manner, for example, they were rude to staff. A lack of confidence in the inspectors' qualifications may lead some teachers to dismiss their judgements and advice, as the following example illustrates:

> *Before they OFSTED-ed us, they asked 'is there any particular references that you need the inspectors to have? Any particular qualifications?' We stated on all our forms that 'there was a language unit with 20 language disordered children in place and they need to send in a specialist who can judge us'. What they sent us was some sort of special needs inspector – but she was for children with additional languages, which is completely different. I was very cynical because I ended up explaining to her the nature of our children's problems and what she was actually looking for. I actually felt she couldn't make a very balanced judgement on how I was doing my job. I'm a qualified speech therapist as well, so I was looking at this and thinking 'well you're inspecting me but on what grounds?'.*

Interview respondents made similar points regarding the conduct of the inspection and professionalism of the OFSTED team. Staff at two special schools were particularly unhappy that the criteria used to judge their schools were the same as those used to judge mainstream schools:

> *I think the OFSTED framework is far too narrow for this sort of establishment. We are working here with some of the most disaffected and disturbed young people. The OFSTED framework – they look at **all** schools by that framework. Our work covers so much more than is covered in that framework. [There is] our therapeutic work, our work with families and the care arrangements for a residential school...I think they should judge the school on the total work of the school.* (Headteacher, School A)

One of these special schools challenged the outcome of the inspection, but its appeal was not successful.

Not all of those interviewed were unhappy with the conduct of the inspection. For example, one teacher described her department's inspector as 'great, very supportive, very realistic', and felt that the overall judgement of the school was fair and accurate. However, the majority of those interviewed (even those who thought the **outcome** was fair) were critical of at least some aspect of the inspection.

b) Shock.

Approximately one-quarter of teachers and over one-fifth of headteachers at special measures schools said they were surprised or shocked by the outcome. Even when respondents were aware of problems and anticipated that the school might be categorised as having serious weakness or requiring special measures, it still came as a shock to have their worst fears confirmed. One of the headteachers interviewed compared it with a bereavement, 'where you know the outcome is inevitable but you still cannot believe it when it actually happens'.

c) Post-OFSTED blues.

The term 'post-OFSTED blues' has come to describe the feelings of exhaustion, burn-out, lack of motivation and even depression which can follow an OFSTED inspection (Ferguson *et al.*, 1999a). Because so much time and effort is put into the preparation, staff may find it difficult to feel motivated once the inspection has actually taken place. In some cases, it can take up to a year for a school to recover its momentum.

Respondents from both samples seemed to have experienced some form of 'post-OFSTED blues', though in special measures schools this may have been a reaction to what lay before them, rather than simply recuperation from the inspection itself. About one-quarter of teachers and just under one-third of headteachers at special measures schools described their sense of depression and despondency after the inspection. Interviews with teachers at schools which are or have been on special measures suggest that these feelings can persist for some time. (This issue is discussed further in Chapter 4.)

The initial reaction to the inspection outcome, reported by over one-half of the headteachers and teachers at **non-special measures** schools, was that the judgement was accurate and fair ('A relatively accurate assessment'). Interestingly, the second most common remark, from over one-fifth of teachers and 17 per cent of heads, was that the inspection was flawed in some way or the outcome was unfair. Their comments here were similar to those made by the special measures group, described earlier. In other respects, however, their responses were quite different to those of the special measures group: for example, fewer than five per cent of heads and teachers said that they were surprised by the outcome.

This chapter has noted the concerns which many respondents (particularly teachers) from special measures schools had about the conduct of their inspection and the accuracy of the outcome. The period after inspection at these schools seems to be traumatic, as teachers and heads try to come to terms with feelings of shock, disappointment and disillusionment. There were considerable differences between special measures and non-special measures schools, and also between teachers and heads, with the latter taking a more positive view of the inspection and its outcome.

The following chapter looks at why schools were put into special measures, the key issues for action identified in their OFSTED reports and school monitoring after inspection.

Chapter 3
Key Issues and Monitoring

3.1 Introduction

All inspection reports identify a number of key issues for action which, according to the inspectors, the school needs to address in order to remedy the weaknesses which have been found at the school. For example, if one of the main findings of the inspection was that attendance levels were low, the corresponding key issue for action might require the school to revise its policy in this area.

Following the publication of each school's inspection report, an action plan which addresses the key issues in the report must be prepared by the school and a copy sent to OFSTED.[5] A school under special measures also has to send its action plan to the Department for Education and Employment (OFSTED, 1999).

The school's plan should give an overview of proposed actions, specify who is responsible for particular actions, identify priorities, set deadlines and identify the resources needed. The action plan should also indicate how progress will be monitored and how it fits in with the existing priorities of the school's development plan (Earley, 1997).

The first part of this chapter looks at the reasons schools were placed under special measures, and the key issues for action identified in the inspection report (for special measures and non-special measures schools). The second part of this chapter looks at school monitoring procedures after the OFSTED inspection.

---

[5] The action plan produced after an OFSTED inspection is referred to as the governors' plan, though in practice it is normally prepared by management and staff (see Ferguson *et al.* 1999).

3.2 Reasons for special measures

The following are the five main reasons schools were placed under special measures, according to heads and teachers:

- Quality of teaching was unsatisfactory. This point was made by 60 per cent of heads and teachers respectively.

- Poor exam results/underachievement. Quality of learning was poor (53 per cent of heads, 42 per cent of teachers).

- Lack of leadership/management problems (44 per cent of heads, 49 per cent of teachers).

- Behaviour and attendance problems (24 per cent of heads, 32 per cent of teachers).

- Problems in implementing the National Curriculum. Curriculum requirements not being met by the school (15 per cent of heads, 13 per cent of teachers).

3.3 Key issues for action

Headteachers at special measures and non-special measures schools were asked to name the three **main** key issues for action identified in the inspection report. The need to improve levels of attainment/exam results was the most frequently mentioned point made by both groups, though the percentage for special measures schools (about two-thirds) was much higher than that for non-SM schools (almost one-half).

Nearly two-thirds of heads at special measures schools reported that the need to improve the quality of teaching was one of the main key issues in their inspection report. Only about one-quarter of heads at non-special measures schools made this point. The need to address management problems is the area where the two groups differ most: only one in ten heads at non-SM schools mentioned improving management, compared with over 40 per cent at SM schools. Given that approximately one-half of headteachers at special measures schools were appointed **after** inspection, it is not surprising to find that management problems was one of the main key issues at these schools.

Improving attainment, implementing the National Curriculum and increasing the amount of assessment were the most frequently mentioned key issues at non-special measures schools.

Headteachers were also asked to what extent they thought the key issues for action identified by the OFSTED inspection team were (a) appropriate, and (b) expected by the school. As Table 3.1 illustrates, the vast majority of headteachers said that most or all of the key issues identified by the inspection team were appropriate. The data suggest that headteachers at non-special measures schools were more likely to have anticipated the key issues for action.

Table 3.1:   Key issues for action

	Schools on special measures	Schools not on special measures
	Heads %	Heads %
Appropriateness:		
All were appropriate	52	34
Most were appropriate	34	50
Fewer than half were appropriate	3	6
A few were appropriate	6	4
None were appropriate	0	0
Do not know	1	1
No response	4	5
Expected:		
All were expected	24	21
Most were expected	32	48
Fewer than half were expected	9	8
A few were expected	13	9
None were expected	6	1
Do not know	7	3
No response	10	10
N*	161	242

Because percentages are rounded to the nearest integer, they may not sum to 100 in all cases.
*Numbers are slightly smaller here because schools inspected pre-1996 were not asked this question.

predicament. The HMI is seen as a critical friend. The following comment illustrates this view:

> *They [HMI inspections] are obviously very stressful, but the HMI inspectors were people that we had a great deal of professional respect for. I suppose because of the job they do, which is going into failing schools and inspecting them, they know what we are up against as well as what they want to see us produce at the end.'* (Teacher)

Special schools, in particular, emphasised that the HMI model was more suitable for that type of school, since they were less disruptive not only for staff, but also for pupils. Both of the special schools which participated in interviews were comparatively small, with the result that there were almost as many inspectors as teaching staff during the week of inspection. This proved to be rather overwhelming for both staff and pupils. The impact of HMI inspections will be discussed further in the following chapter on stress and workload.

3.4.2 LEA and school self-monitoring

The level of LEA and school self-monitoring is likely to increase substantially after special measures is imposed. The different forms and levels of monitoring in special measures and non-special measures schools are discussed below.

Forms of monitoring

Teachers and headteachers were asked to indicate whether the following forms of staff monitoring were in use at their schools:

- observation of teaching;
- checking of documentation prepared by teachers, e.g. lesson plans, paperwork, etc.;
- meetings/interviews regarding progress.

As Table 3.2 shows, the vast majority of respondents (from special measures and non-special measures schools) indicated that all three types of monitoring were in use. There were relatively small differences between the two groups. The figures given by heads were slightly higher than those given by teachers but this is probably because heads have a more complete picture of the range of monitoring at their schools. For example, **all** headteachers said that teaching was monitored, compared with 97 per cent of teachers.

When asked who was responsible for staff monitoring, respondents at special measures and non-special measures schools mentioned a range of people, though headteachers and (to a lesser extent) heads of department were two of the main groups. Not surprisingly, the LEA seemed to take a more active role in staff monitoring in special measures schools. For example nearly one half of headteachers at SM schools, but only around one fifth of those at non-SM schools said that LEA advisors/inspectors monitored teaching.

Table 3.2:   Forms of staff monitoring

	Schools on special measures		Schools not on special measures	
	Heads	*Teachers*	*Heads*	*Teachers*
Forms of monitoring:	%	%	%	%
Observation of teaching	100	97	97	89
Checking documentation	100	97	98	91
Meetings/interviews regarding progress	94	89	93	79
No response	0	0	0	3
N	173	294	255	442

A multiple response question: therefore percentages may not sum to 100.

Levels of monitoring

Headteachers from special measures and non-special measures schools were asked to comment on how monitoring had developed since the last OFSTED inspection. The main point made by both groups was that monitoring had become more systematic and thorough. Monitoring had become a regular feature of the school's work rather than something that was carried out occasionally or half-heartedly. Schools had become more serious about monitoring.

Headteachers and teachers were asked if the amount of staff monitoring had increased since the school's last OFSTED inspection (Table 3.3). Interestingly, the level of

Chapter 4
Stress and Workload

4.1 Factors affecting stress levels

One of the main criticisms of the OFSTED system of school inspection is that it can be extremely stressful for teachers and adds to their already heavy workload. Previous research suggests that the period before the inspection is often more stressful than the inspection itself (Brimblecombe *et al.*, 1996b). A recent ethnographic study of six primary schools identified the particularly stressful elements as: having an inspector in the classroom; negative feedback in the course of the week; concerns over the professional conduct of the OFSTED team; and a general feeling of being 'under surveillance' (Jeffrey and Woods, 1998).

One of the main objectives of the current study was to look at how inspection affected teachers, particularly in terms of staff morale, stress levels and health. In order to investigate these issues, headteachers and teachers were asked to indicate levels of agreement with the following statements on workload and stress levels:

- I feel under uncomfortable pressure because of my workload.
- My job performance has deteriorated as a result of stress in my job.
- I am concerned about my job security at this school.
- I think that I work longer hours each week than do teachers at other schools.

Interestingly, the majority of respondents from **both** special measures and non-special measures groups agreed that they were 'under uncomfortable pressure because of workload' (See Table A4.1 in Appendix 2). Further analysis of the teachers' data revealed that there was a statistically significant relationship between special measures status and agreement with the above statements. Teachers working at special measures schools were more likely to agree with all of these statements, compared with their counter-parts at non-special measures schools.

The results for the headteachers' data were less conclusive. Nearly one half of heads (46 per cent) at non-special measures schools but only 27 per cent of those at special measures schools agreed that their 'job performance has deteriorated as a result of stress'. On the other hand, a significantly higher proportion of headteachers at special measures schools agreed that they were concerned over job security and worked longer hours. One-quarter of headteachers at SM schools were concerned about their job security, compared with only 16 per cent of their counterparts in non-SM schools.

4.2 Stress levels

Teachers were asked to indicate how often they felt 'stressed at work' during the current school year. A higher proportion of teachers at special measures schools reported feeling stressed more frequently than their counterparts in other schools (see Table 4.1 below).

Table 4.1: Experience of stress at work

	Schools on special measures	Schools not on special measures
	Teachers %	Teachers %
Never	1	1
On a few occasions only	8	17
Some of the time	27	43
Most of the time	43	32
All the time	17	4
Don't know	0	0
No response	4	4
N	273	413

Because percentages are rounded to the nearest integer, they may not sum to 100 in all cases.

4.3 Workload

As mentioned above, heads and teachers at special measures schools were more likely to agree with the statement that they 'work longer hours each week than do teachers at other schools'. When asked why they thought they worked longer hours, the main reasons given by respondents at special measures schools were:

- the amount of paperwork they had to do (40 per cent of teachers, 36 per cent of heads);

- lesson preparation (about one-third of teachers);
- the school was under special measures, therefore the workload would be greater than in other schools (over one-quarter of teachers and 40 per cent of headteachers);
- the number of meetings which they had to attend (over one-quarter of teachers and nearly one-fifth of headteachers).

Respondents were also asked to estimate the total number of hours they worked per week during term time, including anything which related to school business (e.g. after school meetings). The average number of hours worked by heads at special measures schools was 63, whilst that for heads at non-special measures schools was 58. Teachers at special measures schools were working an average of 56 hours per week, compared with an average of 53 hours worked by teachers at non-special measures schools.

Interviews with teachers at special measures schools revealed that the nature of their work had changed since inspection, with much of their additional work involving administration or meetings. Some teachers felt that the amount of paperwork required of them was excessive. This point is returned to later in this chapter.

4.4 Illness and time off work

Previous research suggests that the number of teachers suffering from stress-related illnesses increases in the period immediately after inspection. In order to assess the effect of inspection on health, teachers in this survey were asked if they had taken time off due to stress or illness in the six months before or after inspection. Those who did take time off due to illness were also asked how long they took off and whether they considered the inspection to have contributed to their illness. However, in interpreting statistics on time off it must be borne in mind that nearly one-half of heads and one-fifth of teachers did not work at their current school at the time of the OFSTED inspection. Therefore the figures described below do not provide a full picture of levels of absence, especially in the period before inspection.

28

A small proportion of teachers and heads from both samples reported taking time off before their OFSTED inspection. Only two headteachers at special measures schools took time off during this period. These headteachers reported that their illness was not connected with the inspection and that they had taken less than a week off. Four out of the 11 headteachers who had taken time off before inspection at **non-special measures** schools said that their illnesses were connected to the inspection, to varying degrees.[7]

Just over one-tenth (n = 33) of teachers at special measures schools took time off before inspection and 13 of these reported that the inspection had contributed to their illness in some way. A slightly higher percentage (15 per cent) of teachers at non-special measures schools took time off before inspection and just over one-half of these said that the inspection was a contributing factor. The majority of teachers who took time off before inspection (at SM and non-SM schools) said that they had taken three weeks or less.

During the post-inspection period, the figures for time off due to illness increased for both samples, though the figures are noticeably higher for teachers at special measures schools (see Table 4.2 below). Interestingly, the percentage of headteachers who said that the inspection was 'a contributing factor' is higher for non-SM schools than it is for SM schools. Given that the numbers involved are so small (20 heads at SM schools, 37 at non-SM schools), it is difficult to generalise on the reasons for these differences. Furthermore, the interviews suggest that some heads (at SM schools) who took time off due to ill-health never returned to work. They took early retirement or are still on sick leave.

---

[7] Respondents were asked to indicate the degree to which inspection contributed to illness on a scale of one to four, ranging from 'major contributing factor' to 'not connected to inspection in any way'. There was also a 'don't know' option.

Table 4.2:   Time off due to illness/stress

	Schools on special measures		Schools not on special measures	
	Heads %	*Teachers* %	*Heads* %	*Teachers* %
Six months after inspection				
Yes	24	38	17	24
No	75	55	78	66
Not employed in school at that time	0	1	0	0
Don't know	0	1	2	3
No response	1	5	3	7
N*	83	224	219	399

Because percentages are rounded to the nearest integer, they may not sum to 100 in all cases.
*The numbers are slightly lower for this question as it was only directed at schools which were inspected in 1996 or later.

Tables 4.3 and 4.4 show the amount of time taken off during this period and whether it was linked to inspection. It should be noted that the percentages reported in these two tables are based on the number of respondents who took time off, not on the overall sample, hence the lower sample number reported in these tables.

Table 4.3:   Amount of time taken off

	Schools on special measures		Schools not on special measures	
	Heads %	*Teachers* %	*Heads* %	*Teachers* %
Six months after inspection				
Less than a week	60	61	43	65
1–3 weeks	25	32	35	26
4–7 weeks	15	1	14	4
2–4 months	0	2	3	4
Over 4 months	0	2	5	1
No response	0	1	0	0
N*	20	84	37	96

Because percentages are rounded to the nearest integer, they may not sum to 100 in all cases.
*The sample numbers are lower for this question as it was only applicable to respondents who had taken time off.

Table 4.4: **Illness linked to inspection**

	Schools on special measures		Schools not on special measures	
	Heads %	Teachers %	Heads %	Teachers %
Six months after inspection				
Major contributing factor	40	30	35	21
Contributing factor	20	27	38	25
Minor contributing factor	15	12	5	6
Not connected	20	26	19	38
Don't know	5	5	3	9
No response	0	0	0	1
N*	20	84	37	96

Because percentages are rounded to the nearest integer, they may not sum to 100 in all cases.
*The sample numbers are lower for this question as it was only applicable to respondents who had taken time off.

4.5 Most difficult aspects of the special measures process

In order to get a fuller insight into why teachers at special measures schools find the process stressful, interviewees at these schools were asked to describe the most difficult aspects of being under special measures. The results are described below.

- Continuous monitoring.

As indicated in Chapter 3, most of the interview respondents felt that the HMI visits were less disruptive and more helpful than OFSTED inspections. Nevertheless, they did add to teachers' workload and could be stressful, given that so much depends on a successful outcome. The following are some of the interviewees' comments:

> *It still does create stress. As they move on [the HMI inspections], certainly as you get to the fourth and fifth one, people realise that the stakes are a lot higher. For a school in special measures there are only two ways to go – either you come out of special measures or you don't exist. The stakes are much much higher – as time goes on, people realise that.* (Teacher, School C)

> *I think being on special measures is like having a continuous OFSTED. It is not quite so intensive as that but, overall, you know that he is going to come*

back the next term so things have to be pushed forward very rapidly indeed.
There is no leeway for anybody to be ill or go off song slightly. People don't
naturally work absolutely flat out for months at a time. You can do that for a
short time but then people need some breaks and relaxation. (Head, School N)

Added to this, there was both internal and LEA monitoring of teaching, lesson plans
and paperwork. This created a sense of being under constant surveillance which came
as a culture shock in some schools, as the following example illustrates:

Teachers have not got used to it [monitoring] at all. I think they still find it
quite a threatening experience. I think it is because the pressure is on them to
do well. One of the problems here was that nobody had been in for years, the
attached adviser would come in and spend time with the headteacher in the
office and never ventured beyond. The headteacher fed the information that
they wanted to hear. Nobody challenged and so it got very cosy. (New head,
School R)

Similarly, a teacher from another school pointed out that, prior to special measures,
they had rarely had an LEA visitor, but 'now they are hardly ever out of the school'.

- Deprofessionalisation.

In their study on the effects of inspection on primary teachers, Jeffrey and Woods
suggest that the OFSTED system of inspection had 'a latent function of
deprofessionalization'. Based on case-study research in six primary schools, they
suggest that:

Professional uncertainty was induced, with teachers experiencing confusion,
anxiety, professional inadequacy and the marginalization of positive emotions.
They also suffered an assault on their professional selves, closely associated
among primary teachers with their professional roles (Jeffrey and Woods,
1998).

The current study also found that teachers experienced a loss of confidence in their own ability. One teacher pointed out that the worst aspect of being on special measures was 'the constant weight of justification of our **professionality** through paper and provision of paper'. Even respondents whose teaching was acknowledged as good or very good were made to feel inadequate by the whole inspection and special measures process. The feeling that everyone, regardless of the quality of their work, was 'tarred with the same brush' seemed to be one of the most frustrating aspects of inspection. Teachers felt that they were made to suffer even though the problems at the school might have related to factors which were outside their control, such as management issues. As one teacher pointed out, the 'humiliation' would have been easier to deal with if the teachers had been found to be at fault:

> *You are made to feel totally incompetent. You are made to feel that everything you've done for the last 20 years in teaching is absolutely useless. And we still doubt our ability...I think if I had been a failed teacher, I could have accepted it better. But because we knew that it was purely a management issue, that we had done everything we could and more, and yet we still had to suffer the humiliation.* (New head, School M)

At another school, the newly appointed head described the teachers' loss of self-confidence after the inspection:

> *One of the main things that I had to do when I started in September was to work on staff morale. I have to say that there are people who I am still finding on the surface who appear to be okay but you get rumblings... I am still at a stage where I am having to speak to people on an individual basis and say 'yes, you are doing this right'. There were one or two staff here who were virtually destroyed by the OFSTED people. We actually had one member of staff who physically collapsed after one of the Ofsted inspectors had had a go at her.* (Head, School B)

- Labelling.

A related point concerns the 'naming and shaming' of failing schools. 'Public humiliation' was the phrase used by the headteacher at School F, and this sums up what many schools experienced after inspection. Being on special measures often attracts press attention. Interviews revealed that this was front-page headline news in some local papers and that, rather than being a 'one-off' story, negative press coverage continued throughout special measures. In one case, the LEA actually made a complaint to the local newspaper about the continuous coverage.

The stigma of coming from a special measures school manifests itself in a number of ways. For example, teachers may not want to admit that they come from a 'failing' school because (by association) they may be seen as 'failing' teachers:

> It [inspection] *happened in January, I couldn't talk about it until Christmas this year. I only told certain members of my family. I was so humiliated by the whole thing, and if I went on a course, I wouldn't let anyone know where I came from... I couldn't talk about it, it had such a devastating effect.* (Teacher, School M)

The headteacher from another school pointed out that although it was not acceptable to shame pupils into improving their performance, this approach was now being used with teachers:

> I think it [inspection] *is far too negative, we wouldn't do it to children. We wouldn't shame them in order to get them to improve. Yet we do it to teachers and it's OK.* (Head, School K)

However, it is not only school staff who feel stigmatised by inspection. Pupils can also be affected by the labelling process. The headteacher of one school, for example, said that it had always been a problem to motivate the children and being judged a failing school had further undermined their confidence in themselves and their school. In the short term this meant that pupils were putting even less effort into their work.

Respondents from other schools also described the adverse effect of labelling on pupils:

> *I think one of the most difficult aspects is when you are declared a failing school that obviously goes out to the public domain. The school, when it was declared a failing school, got some extremely damaging publicity in the local newspaper. That had a really bad impact on the students. Because* [this] *is a small town, the students got a lot of abuse from students from other schools who were goading them and saying 'they go to a useless school'. That was very difficult to manage. I don't agree with the policy of naming and shaming – I see very little positive in that.* (Head, School H)

> *I don't think* [OFSTED] *is a very productive manner of regulation. I think when schools are OFSTED-ed it knocks them backwards and that does affect the children. If that happens, then the system is not working.* (Teacher, School N)

- Increased workload and type of work.

Teachers' workload increased and the nature of their work changed during special measures. Some respondents complained about excessive paperwork which took them away from what they saw as the real work of teaching. 'Colossal' and 'phenomenal' were two of the words used to describe the level of paperwork at these schools. Teachers felt that at least some of this paperwork was pointless: as one teacher pointed out, it was 'paperwork for paperwork's sake'. Interestingly, interviewees tended not to complain about additional teaching or marking assignments. This could be because these had not increased substantially or because teachers were more willing to accept an increase in this **type** of work. Similarly, in the few instances where teachers complained of having to attend more training courses, it was because this meant that supply staff would have to teach their classes.

The data reported above are based on the interviews. Survey respondents were also asked an open-ended question on the factors which helped to support staff and the factors which discouraged them after the inspection. The support which staff received is discussed in the following chapter, but the main factors which teachers at special measures schools found discouraging were:

- Insufficient support from the LEA;
- The level of LEA monitoring;
- Experience of 'post-OFSTED blues' (see Chapter 2);
- Teachers felt that they were being blamed for the school's failure. Some teachers were made 'scapegoats' by management or other staff.

(Each of the above points was raised by between 15 and 20 per cent of questionnaire respondents.)

All of the above contributed to the stress under which teachers worked during special measures. In some cases, this affected their health or their private lives. For example, a Head of Department at one school simply walked out in the middle of the inspection itself and never came back. In the most extreme cases, heads or teachers were off work for months due to stress-related illness.

The challenges and difficulties of special measures have been outlined in this chapter. The following chapter will look at the support which schools received following inspection and how professional relationships changed.

Chapter 5

Professional Support and Relationships

5.1 Professional support

A number of questions were asked about the support which schools received following their OFSTED inspection. Headteachers and teachers at special measures schools only were asked if additional governors and resources had been allocated to their schools and whether this had been useful (see Tables 5.1 and 5.2 below). Teachers from special measures and non-special measures schools were also asked to indicate how helpful the following people were in providing professional support in the year after the OFSTED inspection:

- The headteacher
- Other members of the Senior Management Team (SMT)
- Middle managers (e.g. Heads of Department, Subject Coordinators, etc.)
- Other teachers
- Governors
- LEA advisers/inspectors
- Other (e.g. outside consultants, other schools).

The results are discussed in the following section and shown in Table A5.1 in Appendix 2. It should be noted that not all respondents were asked the same questions on professional support and relationships: some questions were addressed to either headteachers or teachers, others were addressed to both groups.

The first part of this chapter will look at the professional support provided by the LEA, the governing body and school staff (including the headteacher, SMT and teachers). The second part will look briefly at a related issue: how relationships within the school and between the school and the LEA have changed since the inspection.

5.1.1 LEA support

Previous research (Riley and Rowles, 1997) has found that special measures schools receive additional support from their LEAs, usually in the form of:

- increased funding;
- advice linked to the action plan (including financial expertise and follow-up);
- the provision of extra governors and training for the governing body;
- the identification of seconded teachers, headteachers or advisers to play a role in the school over a period of time;
- the Director of Education taking a direct personal interest.

Some LEAs set up a special budget for schools requiring special measures. LEAs also have the option of withdrawing delegated funding, though as Riley and Rowles have pointed out, such action may undermine the school's belief in its own capacity to improve.

The current research found that, in most cases, the LEA provided additional resources or funding when schools were placed under special measures, and comparatively few schools had their budgets withdrawn (see Table 5.1 below). It must be borne in mind that teachers' replies, reported below, do not reflect the percentage of **schools** which have been given additional help, as more than one teacher at a particular school could have responded. The headteachers' data give a more accurate reflection of the number of schools receiving help from their LEAs as only one headteacher response would have been received from each school.

Respondents were also asked if they found this additional support helpful. The results are shown in Table 5.2. The majority of respondents found the allocation of additional resources helpful, but the findings from the small number of schools that experienced a withdrawal of the delegated budget were less positive.

Table 5.1:   LEA actions following special measures

Schools on special measures

	Heads %	Teachers %
Appointment of additional governors		
Yes	57	37
No	36	31
Don't know	1	19
Not applicable	5	6
No response	1	6
Allocation of additional resources		
Yes	85	70
No	9	8
Don't know	1	12
Not applicable	2	5
No response	3	5
Withdrawal of the delegated budget		
Yes	13	10
No	79	45
Don't know	1	31
Not applicable	4	6
No response	5	9
N	173	294

Table 5.2:   Usefulness of LEA actions

Schools on special measures

	Heads %	Teachers %
Appointment of additional governors		
Helpful	79	50
Neither helpful nor unhelpful	17	41
Unhelpful	2	3
Do not know	1	6
No response	1	0
N*	98	109
Allocation of additional resources		
Helpful	95	86
Neither helpful nor unhelpful	3	9
Unhelpful	0	1
Do not know	1	4
No response	2	1
N*	147	205
Withdrawal of the delegated budget		
Helpful	36	22
Neither helpful nor unhelpful	41	21
Unhelpful	18	21
Do not know	0	36
No response	5	0
N*	22	28

Because percentages are rounded to the nearest integer, they may not sum to 100 in all cases.
*The sample numbers are lower for this question as it was only applicable to respondents who answered 'yes' to one or more of the comments listed in Table 5.1.

helpful. The similarities between the two datasets here suggest that teachers and governors do not necessarily work more closely because of the imposition of special measures.

5.1.3 Support from other school staff

Teachers (from special measures and non-special measures schools) were also asked to comment on how helpful the following members of staff were in providing professional support after the inspection: the headteacher; the Senior Management Team; middle managers; and other teachers. There were no striking differences between the two samples (see Table A5.1 in Appendix 2 for details). The majority of teachers said that the headteacher, the SMT and middle managers had been helpful, but 'other teachers' emerged as the single most important group with about 70 per cent of respondents from both samples reporting that their colleagues were helpful/very helpful in providing support. The following are some of the comments from headteachers at special measures schools: 'The whole school was united with a common goal.' 'Staff pulled together in adversity.'

Teachers were also asked an open-ended question on any other factors which helped to support them after the inspection. Team spirit and mutual support were mentioned by about one-third of respondents, followed by the appointment of a new headteacher (14 per cent). After schools were placed on special measures, staff worked more closely together, and appeared to be united in the face of adversity, as the following comments illustrate:

> *No matter what, when OFSTED failed the school in December, all the staff pulled together and they were together in it.* (Teacher)

> *Mutual support, very strong teamwork.* (Teacher)

> *Good sense of humour and friendship, and a commitment to the school and each other.* (Teacher)

About one-tenth of teachers mentioned support from the LEA and from parents respectively.

5.2 Relationships

A related issue is how relationships between different groups changed since before the inspection process began. Heads and teachers were asked to indicate whether their relationship with others had improved or deteriorated since before the whole process of the last OFSTED inspection had begun, i.e. before the school was notified of the inspection. Respondents were asked to answer this question even if there had been staff changes at the school. The objective was to look at whether relationships between different groups (e.g. headteachers and the LEA) had changed, regardless of whether the individuals in these posts had changed. Heads and teachers were asked to comment on the relationship:

- Between the SMT and other teaching staff
- Between the headteacher and teaching staff
- Amongst teaching staff
- Between teaching staff (including SMT) and governors
- Between teaching staff (including SMT) and pupils
- Between teaching staff (including SMT) and parents
- Between the school and the LEA
- Within the SMT (headteachers' questionnaire only)
- Between head and governors (headteachers' questionnaire only).

The results are shown in Tables A5.2(a) and A5.2(b) in Appendix 2. Changes in professional relationships are more evident at special measures schools. Overall, where relationships had changed, they are more likely to have improved rather than to have deteriorated. For example, seven per cent of teachers at special measures schools said that their relationship with parents had deteriorated since inspection, but more than four times that number (31 per cent) said that it had improved. Another relationship which seems to have undergone significant change is that between special measures schools and their LEAs: 57 per cent of heads and 45 per cent of teachers reported an improvement.

However, in some cases, a sizeable **minority** reported a deterioration in relationships (see Table A5.2). For example, although 44 per cent of teachers at special measures schools reported an improvement in the relationship with the head, about one-fifth said that this relationship had deteriorated. Their comments indicated that where a deterioration in the relationship between staff and management had occurred, this was usually because teachers did not agree with certain initiatives/policies, or because the additional workload was creating tensions:

> *The pressure being placed on the head to meet targets by HMI in order to get schools out of special measures has resulted in a succession of new initiatives creating excessive workload in a school with a small staff. Many staff often feel they are not able to meet targets and so feel failures.* (Teacher)

> *Relationships between the headteacher and staff [are] bound to deteriorate due to measures needed to improve the school associated with staffing issues.* (Head)

A failed inspection could also cause divisions amongst the teaching staff themselves. Some teachers or departments were seen to have 'passed', whilst others had failed. The following are some examples of the initial resentment and tensions created after the inspection:

> *The atmosphere after the OFSTED, once they had left us with this special measures, was appalling. As [my] unit had done well, it was very much a case of 'well you're alright, you don't need to worry about it'. It got to a point where I was thinking I really can't bear being in this staffroom because there is this element 'well you're alright but we're not'. We've worked through it now. We got together and said we are all in the same boat – the school's got to improve or they will close all of us down. We came through that but there were a few months there where it was all very unpleasant and I don't think it was that necessary to do it that way.* (Teacher, School O)

In the nursery the inspectors said that every lesson they saw was either good or better. I am astounded that they said that about it. I think that either they got a very good week over there or they [OFSTED] *didn't use the same criteria. That did cause some divisiveness as you can imagine that the nursery teacher has a view that this is nothing to do with her – 'If you are as good as me, you would have been alright'. What happened in the meantime is that as the other staff have worked their socks off she hasn't worked her socks off.*
(Headteacher, School D)

This report has so far looked at the experience of special measures, support for staff during this time and changes to relationships. The final chapter, based on Survey 1 data, will look at the outcomes and effects of the whole inspection process.

The greater progress reported at special measures schools (compared to other schools) may be partly due to the additional support and funding they received. Regular monitoring by the HMI and the threat of closure are two other (less welcome) incentives to change. Furthermore, there may be more scope for improvement at special measures schools. The reasons for progress in special measures schools are looked at in greater detail in a later section.

6.1.2 Deterioration

There were also some aspects of school life which seem to have deteriorated since inspection. This was most notable in relation to *Staff morale*, as reported by teachers from both groups of schools (see Table 6.2 below). The percentage of teachers at special measures schools who felt that staff morale had deteriorated (58 per cent) is over twice the number who thought it had improved. The contrast is even greater in non-special measures schools, where nearly one-half of the teachers reported a deterioration compared with only 11 per cent reporting an improvement. This figure is not entirely surprising, as schools generally can experience 'post-OFSTED blues' in the year after inspection (Ferguson *et al.*, 1999a). Table 6.2 also indicates that opinion **within** the special measures group was quite divided. Although heads were more positive than teachers about the effects of the inspection, there seemed to be little consensus within the headteachers' group. Whereas nearly one-third of heads at special measures schools said that staff morale had deteriorated, another 50 per cent said that it had improved.

Table 6.2:   Effects of the inspection process

		Schools on special measures		Schools not on special measures	
		Heads %	Teachers %	Heads %	Teachers %
Staff morale					
	Improved	50	25	17	11
	No change	11	9	40	36
	Deteriorated	32	58	36	48
	Unable to say	2	5	3	3
	No response	5	4	4	3
School's reputation in the community					
	Improved	41	30	35	28
	No change	24	25	51	51
	Deteriorated	26	35	7	10
	Unable to say	6	9	4	7
	No response	3	2	3	4
Schools ability to recruit staff					
	Improved	17	-	9	-
	No change	36	-	73	-
	Deteriorated	36	-	9	-
	Unable to say	8	-	5	-
	No response	3	-	4	-
Schools ability to retain staff					
	Improved	21	-	5	-
	No change	46	-	80	-
	Deteriorated	24	-	7	-
	Unable to say	7	-	4	-
	No response	3	-	4	-
N		173	294	255	442

Because percentages are rounded to the nearest integer, they may not sum to 100 in all cases.

Reputation in the community is an area in which special measures schools were more likely than non-SM schools to report a deterioration. However, the results were somewhat inconclusive: about one-third of teachers said that the school's reputation had deteriorated, around another third said that it had improved, whilst one-quarter reported no change.

As Table 6.2 indicates, special measures schools were more likely to report a deterioration rather than an improvement in their ability to recruit staff. Approximately equal numbers of heads at special measures schools reported an improvement or deterioration in their schools' ability to retain staff. Staffing issues are discussed further in the following section.

6.2 Changes in staffing

Schools on special measures often experience an increase in staff turnover, before and after the inspection. Staff may decide to seek work elsewhere or retire. In some cases, staff are made redundant or dismissed.

One indicator of the level of change is the number of respondents who were in the school for the last inspection. As Table 6.3 shows, only about one-half of the headteachers at special measures schools worked at their current school (either as head or in another role) during the last OFSTED inspection. About one-fifth of teachers at special measures schools were not employed at their current school during the last inspection.

Table 6.3:   Working in school at time of inspection

	Schools on special measures		Schools not on special measures	
	Heads %	Teachers %	Heads %	Teachers %
Yes, as headteacher	44	-	83	-
Yes	5	80	7	96
No	49	19	10	4
No response	2	1	0	0
N	173	294	255	442

Because percentages are rounded to the nearest integer, they may not sum to 100 in all cases.

In order to obtain more detailed information headteachers were asked about staff changes. Respondents were asked to compare teaching staff figures in the year before inspection with those for the year after inspection and indicate whether there had been a change in the average number of the following:

- Teaching staff
- New appointments
- Average number of applicants for each new appointment
- Resignations
- Retirement on grounds of ill-health
- Other retirements
- Redundancies

- Competency/disciplinary procedures
- Dismissals
- Staff sick leave (days per year).

The results are shown in Tables A6.2(a) and A6.2(b) in Appendix 2. Not surprisingly, the results show that there is far more stability in non-special measures schools. Differences between the two groups are most evident for resignations, retirements on grounds of ill-health and competency/disciplinary procedures. Just over one-third of respondents at SM schools indicated that the number of retirements on grounds of ill-health had increased, whereas only 12 per cent of those at non-SM schools made this point. Similarly, the number of respondents reporting an increase in resignations at SM schools (45 per cent) is more than twice that reported for non-special measures schools. These results bear out interview accounts that during special measures staff may look for work elsewhere or are forced to leave the school.

The figures on increases in dismissals is comparatively low (11 per cent), though again, the interview data suggest that teachers and heads sometimes leave, rather than waiting to be dismissed or going through competency/disciplinary procedures. One teacher (who was broadly in favour of the special measures process) summed up the situation in his school following inspection:

> *It was very dramatic in the sense that the weak people went to the wall and we lost half our Heads of Department. The people who were told that their teaching was weak realised that they had been found out and couldn't hack it any more and left for one reason or another.* (Teacher, School L)

When asked about the circumstances under which these staff left, the teacher reported that 'a couple had nervous breakdowns and a couple just left'.

In some cases, teachers who were considered to be competent or good at their jobs also left because of the stress of the inspection or they did not want to go through the special measures process. These teachers looked for jobs elsewhere or took early retirement. The special measures label also made it difficult for some schools to recruit and retain staff:

> *When I advertised a language and technology post, I have had no applicants. I have a good lot here at the moment, but because of the threat of reorganisation, and together with the pressure of special measures, my good staff are getting jobs and I can't replace them ... Given the choice, would you go and work in a school with special measures or in one in the leafy suburbs?*
>
> (Headteacher)

The findings on increases in disciplinary/competency procedures were quite striking, with 51 per cent of heads at special measures schools reporting an increase in the year following inspection (see Table A6.2(b) in Appendix 2).

6.3 Achieving school improvement

The contrast between declining staff morale and improvements in the quality of education reported earlier in this chapter is one of the most interesting results of this and other questions in the survey: there would appear to be an inverse relationship between the two variables. Ferguson *et al.* (1999a) have summed up the dilemma faced by special measures schools:

> *In some ways it could be seen to be an advantage to be put into the category of 'serious weaknesses' or 'special measures' because the additional support and resources that are made available make it much easier for significant progress to be made. Those in this position are, however, unlikely to perceive things in this way and the public labelling of schools means that improvement is often achieved at the cost of a great deal of unhappiness and some heads and staff are left with feelings of resentment long after the inspection is over. Whether or not this is in the best interests of pupils, in the long or the short term, is a matter of ongoing debate.*

The issue of school improvement was explored in detail through interviews with staff at schools which were (or had been) on the special measures register. In most cases, the heads and teachers who were interviewed reported that improvements had taken place during special measures. Interviewees were asked what they were basing their judgements on and the majority mentioned positive feedback from the HMI or the LEA, and their own observations of what was happening in the school. In some cases, there had also been improvements in test/exam results. Improvements were mainly attributed to one or more of the following:

- changes in management;
- increased funding and advisory support;
- the focus and urgency which the special measures process entails.

Each of these points is looked at below.

6.3.1 Changes in management

In the majority of schools at which interviews were held, there had been a change of headship either in the year before or after inspection. Headteachers left under various circumstances: they were asked to leave, following the imposition of special measures; they took extended sick leave from which they had not returned; they retired early; or they were due to retire/leave the school anyway. The exact role which inspection played in the departure of headteachers is not always clear because, as one teacher governor pointed out, many 'behind the scenes' decisions were made.

With one exception, where the deputy head was promoted, all the new headteacher appointments were made from outside the school.

In almost all cases, a change at management level was seen as leading to school improvement. The appointment of new headteachers seemed to give schools a greater sense of direction. Although staff in some schools felt sorry for what had happened to their previous head, in most cases they seemed to accept the new management. The following example is taken from a school which had appointed a replacement headteacher whilst the permanent head was on extended sick leave:

The whole situation is terribly sad, we have still got our loyalties to our head, but it is nice to know that we are going to be going forward and he [the new head] assures us that we are all going to get ourselves out of special measures. That gives you a very positive angle. (Teacher, School I)

Whilst new headteachers (that is, those appointed in the year before or after inspection) were often critical of the special measures process, their replies suggested that it had strengthened their own position in the school and allowed them to take actions which might not have been possible under other circumstances. In some cases, this meant removing staff who were seen as incompetent. Special measures became a cathartic process, as the following example illustrates:

It also led to the fact that I was able to ease out of the school some long-standing but less effective teachers and I don't think I'd have been able to do that without actually having to have the damage of the OFSTED inspection. The LEA, the year prior to the change in the teachers' pension arrangements, actually was able to support a number of early retirements and that enabled me to bring in quite a large number of new, young, enthusiastic heads of department. (New head, School L)

6.3.2 Additional resources and advisory support

Apart from changes at management level, the allocation of additional resources to the school was the other important change during special measures. Some teachers expressed surprise at the amount of money which was suddenly being made available to their schools:

The most important thing to my point of view is the fact that it actually opened doors to extra support, both financial and adviser support. You can ask for things from county that they don't give to every school but because your school is in special measures you can get it. I have told other people whose schools are teetering on the brink not to worry and that it isn't the end of the world, although it feels like it at the time. (Teacher, School L)

We had an awful lot of money poured into the school – money for resources, for example, computer equipment. ICT was one of the areas criticised, as was design technology and music ... There was a lot more money for staff development – courses, etc. The OFSTED report obviously led to this. It led to the support by county, which facilitated the money into the school. (Teacher, School N)

The headteacher at another school pointed out that because of the level of support they received, being put into special measures was ultimately more advantageous than being classed a 'serious weakness' school:

I had only been in post for six months at the time of the inspection, so obviously I viewed it as being a good way of taking the school forward. I didn't think the school was special measures, but I did feel there were serious weaknesses. The outcome of it, being in special measures, has meant that the support received is far greater than being in serious weaknesses. There is also now the chance of coming out of that category. I don't think with serious weaknesses that is the case – because you stay in serious weaknesses until you are re-inspected which could be four years. Being in special measures you do have that opportunity to come right out. We did discuss with the team, which was going to be better (serious weaknesses or special measures) for me personally and whilst special measures was a bitter pill for everybody to swallow it has meant that the resourcing has come in from the authority. The support has been there and it has focused everybody's minds dramatically. (Head, School R)

Interestingly, in the above example, the inspectors seem to have consulted with the head on whether special measures or serious weaknesses would have been more useful for her.

In some schools, additional funding was used to employ extra staff. At one special school, for example, the number of teaching staff almost trebled in the post-OFSTED period. According to the headteacher, this was the main factor in helping the school to improve.

(The importance of additional support was also reflected in the responses to a survey question on what additional resources or changes were necessary for the school to be removed from special measures. See Appendix 2 for details.)

6.3.3 Focusing minds

The idea that inspection had 'focused minds' was mentioned in numerous interviews. Respondents felt that whilst OFSTED might not always have told them something new, special measures concentrated their energies in particular areas or, in some cases, speeded up changes which were already taking place. However, teachers did not necessarily feel that special measures had focused their energies correctly. This is discussed further in the following section.

6.4 Did the ends justify the means?

Whilst acknowledging that improvements had been made, most of those interviewed felt that there were better and more cost-effective ways of achieving the same ends. It was felt that whilst the process had addressed some problems, it had also created new problems or aggravated existing ones. In this sense, the role of OFSTED in school improvement can be contradictory and counter-productive. An example from one of the primary schools at which interviews were held should illustrate this point.

At School F the inspectors had found ineffective management to be at the root of the school's problems. Subsequently, the headteacher left, the deputy was promoted and there was an almost immediate improvement at the school. However, being on special measures had created a number of new problems which the school now had to pour all its energies into addressing. This included: dealing with the public humiliation of being labelled a 'failing' school; a strained relationship with parents and the community; and the continuous monitoring from the LEA and HMI. Because most teachers had been given good grades for their teaching, monitoring was even more onerous in this school. Although OFSTED had praised the work of the majority of teachers, its subsequent actions undermined confidence and created what were felt to be unnecessary pressures on staff. In this way, whilst OFSTED had been instrumental in removing a weak headteacher, even more progress at the school might have been achieved if the school had not had to go through the special measures process. The headteacher pointed out that:

To have people come in and put the school into special measures, I can understand why they have to do that. I can understand it was a mechanism to get rid of the head. Now I can understand that to move a school forward, very often a head has to go. But I really feel that there should be some way of getting rid of management and sorting it out without the rest of the staff suffering like we have suffered.

She went on to suggest that management problems should be tackled by the LEA, not by the inspection process:

Because it was weak management, nothing could be done. We were absolutely helpless. We had the evidence but nothing would be done. The LEA must bear some of the blame in not coming in. The LEA knew what was going on... The LEA used the excuse that we are a [denominational] school and therefore they have limited access or limited control. But nobody seemed to do anything. Nobody seemed to take any action and we were left struggling trying to do the best we could for these children.

The new headteacher at another school made a similar point regarding the need for management problems to be tackled by the LEA, not by the inspection process:

As I wasn't here when it went into special measures, you could say the inspection process forced the previous head out, rightly or wrongly, and forced in the new head [the interviewee] *and we were forced to go through changes because of that process. My argument would be the LEA should be monitoring schools, as most LEAs are, properly, so that those weaknesses are identified, and you shouldn't need an expensive 'snapshot' inspection process to point out things later. Kids are suffering in the interim. Kids here suffered, in OFSTED terms, for three years. Whereas if the LEA was doing their job properly – monitoring schools and making schools evaluate the work they were doing – then standards wouldn't have dropped in the first place.*
(Headteacher, School J)

In schools where a head was appointed in the year **before** the inspection, some staff questioned the rationale/benefit of special measures as they felt the new head had not been given sufficient time to implement change. As reported in an earlier chapter, these heads felt that they had already identified the problems and were taking steps to address them. Furthermore, although special measures 'focused minds', respondents felt that these improvements would have probably taken place anyway. There was a feeling in schools which had already appointed new headteachers that inspection and special measures accelerated change rather than being a real catalyst for the change. For example, at one school where a new head was appointed before the inspection, the inspectors commented on the improvements which had been made – 'the green shoots of recovery'. However, the headteacher felt that:

The effect of inspection initially was to almost stamp out those green shoots of recovery because of the damage which it did to us personally and I would argue that we would probably be in almost as good a position now if we hadn't had the inspection. What the inspection did, though, was actually to bring in a level of support from the LEA and I guess helped focus our minds

58

perhaps in a way that we were able to implement change so speedily. (New head, School L)

In cases where the allocation of additional resources or the employment of additional staff was the key factor in improving standards, teachers asked why this could not have been done earlier and without the trauma of special measures. Some pointed out that it was ironic that so much money was being used on inspection, which could have been used directly on school improvement, for example, by employing more teachers.

It was mentioned earlier in this chapter, that there were some aspects of school life which seem to have deteriorated substantially since inspection, most notably staff morale. Chapter 4, on stress and workload, outlines why teachers found the special measures process difficult and demoralising therefore this will not be described in detail here. However, it is worth mentioning that some teachers felt that creating a demoralised teaching staff is not the correct route to school improvement. As one teacher pointed out, the 'human cost' was too great:

> *But the real concern for me is that we seem to be forgetting, in the education system and a lot of other systems in this country, is that human beings are the ones who do the work and human beings are the clients. We're not just dealing with machinery, we're dealing with human beings, and there is a huge human cost involved in all of this. To see people leaving the teaching profession permanently following an OFSTED, it's no good. I've seen people go through the most awful processes.* (Teacher, School E)

A similar point has been raised in the literature on school improvement. Some commentators have argued that, if change is imposed on a school from outside (for example, through inspection), teachers may lack a sense of 'ownership' of the process. They suggest that unless schools are able to do things for themselves, then any changes are likely to be superficial:

> *For many commentators, self-evaluation is the crucial mechanism for achieving any kind of school improvement. Underpinning everything is said to*

be questions of ownership and empowerment. School improvement has to be in the hands of teachers and other stakeholders and this, it is claimed, is unlikely to be promoted by top-down directives or an inspectorial approach to development (Earley *et al.*, 1998).

Most of those interviewed felt that whilst improvements had been made, there were better ways of achieving the same ends. Broadly speaking, the majority of respondents were in favour of some aspects of the special measures process (for example, extra funding and advisory support, change in leadership), but they did not support the catalyst for change, that is the OFSTED inspection itself. However a few respondents did feel that their schools needed the shock of failing an inspection to bring about improvement. For this reason, they were generally in favour of both the inspection **and** the special measures process. As one teacher pointed out, the school needed 'a good shake-up'.

It should be pointed out, at this stage, that none of the teachers interviewed opposed school inspection as such, in fact most of them were quite vehement in their view that accountability was necessary in education. They objected to OFSTED because, in their view, it seemed to create as many problems as it solved. Their main suggestions for improving the system of inspection are outlined below. Where appropriate, comparisons with the House of Commons Select Committee findings are made.

- Respondents were in favour of an inspection system that would provide more than a 'snapshot' view of the school. They felt that the current system of a one-week inspection every four years does not give a very realistic picture of the school and is unnecessarily stressful. Inspection needs to be more thorough and professional:

One of the things that is very difficult is to actually get staff to accept that these people are expert enough to go in and see, very often, less than half a lesson. If the feedback is negative it is far more difficult to get staff to accept it if the observation has only been for part of a lesson... The staff feel devalued – if you are going to be observing people properly and professionally I think

60

there ought to be the courtesy of actually being there for the beginning and the end of the lesson. (Head, School B)

- A related point is the idea that the period of notice prior to inspection should be shorter. Again, this would make the inspection more realistic and prevent the months of preparation and anticipation which are often the most difficult aspects of inspection:

  I think a lot of the current system is manufactured. When you get your OFSTED inspection – telling people three or six months in advance that it is going to happen, it gives the management time to screw everybody down. I would sooner they say 'we're going to come next month' because then you have to explain what you are doing. I think there is too much reliance put on documentation and less reliance put on knowledge. I don't write everything down. (Teacher, School B)

(OFSTED announced in 1999 that the period of notice will be reduced to between six and ten weeks.)

- Inspection should have an advisory, supportive function rather than simply that of judging the school. Most interviewees preferred the HMI system whereby someone inspects the school but also offers advice and support. On the other hand, the OFSTED model seemed to offer surveillance without support. A similar issue was raised as part of the House of Commons Select Committee hearings on the work of OFSTED. They noted that:

  We therefore do not agree...that OFSTED inspectors should always provide advice per se *based on their inspection findings. Neither do we believe that schools are best served by the pure audit model of inspection – the trenchant critique of a school's strengths and weaknesses and nothing else* (House of Commons Education and Employment Committee, 1999).

- Self-evaluation should play a greater part in school improvement:

I think the current inspection system is deprofessionalising teachers. I would much more like to see a more collaborative system than we have now... *Schools are trying to con the [OFSTED] inspectors and not give them a true picture. I would like to see more emphasis on in-service training, particularly for management on schools' self-evaluation. The inspection ought to be a kind of moderation process.* (Head, School D)

The House of Commons Select Committee enquiry on the work of OFSTED also recommended that:

...the Inspection Framework be amended to take account of the self-evaluation procedures used by schools. Inspection should include assessment of the contribution that self-evaluation is making to standards of achievement. This should be the case in both short and full inspections (GB. Parliament. HoC. Education and Employment Committee, 1999).

- There should be prevention rather than cure. Some respondents pointed out that the problems which put them into special measures could have been addressed beforehand, for example, by more support from their LEA. Schools should be offered support before rather than after the inspection.

- The criteria used to judge special schools should not be the same as those used to judge mainstream schools. This was an issue on which the Select Committee also expressed concern:

A rigorous and appropriate approach is needed to the inspection of special schools. The Inspection Framework needs to be applied in a way which takes account of the genuinely special nature of special education and the varying aims of different kinds of special schools and their aspirations for different children at the school. Given the importance of this issue, we recommend that OFSTED keep under review the way in which the Framework is used in the inspection of special schools (GB. Parliament. HoC. Education and Employment Committee, 1999).

The inspection procedures have changed over the last year and a revised Framework is due for publication. From January 2000 a differential system of inspection will come into operation whereby some schools will have a short or 'light-touch' inspection:

> *The criteria for determining whether a school will have a short inspection will take account of a range of factors including, but not limited to, pupils' academic achievement. Those criteria will be reviewed in the light of experience and as more data about schools and pupils' achievements become available* ... (GB. Parliament. HoC. Education and Employment Committee, 1999).

The system of OFSTED inspections is therefore still evolving and likely to undergo further change in the next few years.

This chapter has considered the various effects of inspection and special measures with particular reference to school improvement and staff morale. The final two chapters will look at the findings from schools which have been removed from special measures (Survey 2).

Chapter 7

Experience of Former Special Measures Schools

A second survey was carried out of schools which have been removed from the special measures register. This survey was smaller in scale, consisting of 134 primary, 33 secondary and 29 special schools. The survey was administered in exactly the same way and at the same time as Survey 1. The questionnaires were sent to headteachers and either two or four teachers (depending on phase of schooling). Questionnaires were distributed by the headteacher, and two reminder letters were sent.

Background information on the respondents (gender, position in school etc.) is given in Appendix 1.

Table 7.1:   Response rate

	No. of questionnaires sent	*No. of questionnaires returned*	*Response rate*
Heads	196	88	45%
Teachers	458	132	29%
Total	654	220	34%

7.1 Aims of Survey 2

The main aims of the survey were to look at:

- the factors which were significant in helping schools come out of special measures;

- the advice they would offer to schools currently on the special measures register;

- how schools changed during special measures and whether they changed **after** the school's removal from the register.

Some of the questions put to the Survey 2 respondents were the same as those used for Survey 1. These comprised:

- views on the outcome of inspection;

- stress and workload;

- the professional support which schools received during special measures;

- the effects of the inspection process.

In general, responses to these questions were broadly similar for both surveys, though any comparisons are made tentatively, as the numbers involved in Survey 2 are relatively small (see Table 7.1).

7.2 Outcome of the inspection

A comparison of the findings on whether the outcome of the inspection was a fair reflection of the quality of education at the school did not reveal any substantial differences between Survey 1 and 2 respondents. For example, the percentage of teachers who felt that the outcome was fair was exactly the same for the two groups (30 per cent). (See Table 7.2 below and Table 2.1, Chapter 2 for further details.)

Table 7.2: **Inspectors' judgement of the school**

	Heads %	Teachers %
Much too positive	0	0
Too positive	0	0
A fair reflection	43	30
Too negative	18	24
Much too negative	21	26
Unable to say	2	10
No response	16	11
N	84	121

Because percentages are rounded to the nearest integer, they may not sum to 100 in all cases.

Like their Survey 1 counterparts, schools no longer on special measures reported that their initial reactions to failing their inspection were: shock; a belief that the inspection was unfair or partial in some way; and feelings of disappointment and despondency ('post-OFSTED blues'). The reasons given for the imposition of special measures were also quite similar for both groups and included: problems with management; quality of teaching; and poor exam results/levels of attainment.

Headteachers included in Surveys 1 and 2 were asked to what extent they thought the key issues for action identified by the OFSTED inspection team were (a) appropriate and (b) expected by the school. The majority from both groups said that most or all of the key issues were appropriate. The percentage who said that the key issues were expected was lower for Survey 2 respondents, though it is difficult to make comparisons because about one-fifth of this group did not reply or indicated that they did not know (see Table A7.1 in Appendix 3 for details).

7.3 Stress, workload and working environment

Respondents to both Surveys 1 and 2 were asked to indicate their level of agreement with each of the following statements[8]:

- I feel under uncomfortable pressure because of my workload.
- My job performance has deteriorated as a result of stress in my job.
- I am concerned about my job security at this school.

---

[8] On a scale of 1 (Strongly agree) to 4 (Strongly disagree), with an additional 'Don't know' category.

- I think that I work longer hours each week than do teachers at other schools.

Not surprisingly, respondents from schools which have been removed from special measures were less likely to agree with the above statements than their Survey 1 counterparts. This was particularly evident in concerns over job security, where 42 per cent of Survey 1 teachers were concerned, compared with only 22 per cent for those at schools which were no longer on special measures. The statement on which there was the highest level of agreement was that on pressures caused by workload, with 83 per cent of Survey 1 and 75 per cent of Survey 2 teachers agreeing. (The Survey 2 results are shown in Table A7.2 in Appendix 3; the Survey 1 results are shown in Table A4.1 in Appendix 2 and described in detail in Chapter 4.)

Differences in levels of stress reported by Survey 1 and 2 respondents are shown in Table 7.3 below. Workload and stress are discussed further in the following section.

Table 7.3:   **Levels of stress at work**

	Survey 2 Teachers %	Survey 1 Teachers %
Never	1	1
On a few occasions only	12	8
Some of the time	46	27
Most of the time	35	43
All the time	3	17
Don't know	0	0
No response	3	4
N	121	273

Because percentages are rounded to the nearest integer, they may not sum to 100 in all cases.

7.4 Changes following the removal of special measures

Chapters 2 – 6 looked at the experience of special measures, and how schools and the professional lives of teachers changed during this period. Increased workload, stress and feelings of 'deprofessionalisation' were some of the main findings. In order to find out whether their professional life changed following the removal of special measures, Survey 2 respondents (teachers and heads) were asked to indicate whether the following had increased, decreased or stayed the same:

- average number of hours you work per week
- your level of stress at work
- average number of days you take off due to illness
- your level of job satisfaction
- confidence in your job security
- amount of LEA monitoring of the school
- amount of school's self-monitoring.

In addition, headteachers only were asked whether there had been an increase or reduction in the following, after the school was removed from special measures:

- number of applications for teaching posts
- amount of governing body involvement in the school
- amount of parental involvement in the school
- amount of financial support/resources which the school receives
- number of applicants for pupil places.

There were some areas where substantial improvements had been made to teachers' lives (e.g. reduction in stress levels). In other areas change was less evident (average hours worked) and in a small number of cases, there had been a deterioration of some aspect of school life. These findings are discussed further below and shown in Tables A7.3(a) and A7.3(b) in Appendix 3.

The majority of teachers (57 per cent) and over one-third of heads (38 per cent) reported that stress levels had decreased since the removal of special measures. Their comments indicate the relief felt at these schools, for example: 'I felt that a nightmare was over! I felt that a proper decision had justly been made'.

Levels of job satisfaction and (to a lesser extent) confidence in job security also increased following the removal of special measures. Phrases such as 'satisfaction, feeling valued' were used by respondents providing further comments. One teacher pointed out:

> *My job satisfaction improved, because I felt I'd achieved a personal goal, as well as within a team.*

Another head who had indicated that his job satisfaction had increased significantly added that, 'I finally feel I am in charge of the running of the school'.

Not having regular HMI inspections was also instrumental in reducing workload and stress:

> *Welcome opportunity to not have to keep evidence of every initiative and improvement, which was required by HMI, but did nothing to move the school forward. Staff look forward to not being made to feel constantly 'unworthy' through criticisms by HMI.* (Head)

However, as Table A7.3(a) shows, 37 per cent of teachers and 56 per cent of heads said that stress levels had either remained the same or increased since the removal of special measures. They were now under pressure to maintain the improvements which had been made and they could still have occasional HMI visits. The following are some of their comments:

> *Despite being out of special measures, the pressure was on to maintain the high standard that had been achieved. The knowledge that an HMI would return kept stress levels high.* (Teacher)

> *Coming out of special measures saw little change on the whole – it was the going in that 'revved' everything up. All staff giving 100 per cent plus the rest – this hasn't really abated in most areas.* (Head)

A sizeable proportion of heads and teachers reported that there had been no change to some aspects of school life. This was particularly evident in the average number of hours worked, the levels of school self-monitoring and days off due to illness. Over 50 per cent of heads and teachers indicated that the average number of hours they worked per week had not changed. Where a decrease in hours worked was reported, it was almost always a 'slight' rather than a 'significant' decrease. Comments made by some respondents shed further light on this. For example, although special measures have been removed, serious underlying problems remain which schools must continue to address:

The school, though no longer on the special measures register, still has serious weaknesses (although not in official category of serious weakness schools), so momentum on all fronts has been maintained. Weaknesses still in the quality of teaching and assessment. (Head)

The realisation that the pressure never stops and that we will always be 'vulnerable', i.e. 60 per cent SEN, falling rolls, poor funding. (Head)

Although the level of LEA monitoring appears to have decreased in the majority of cases, school self-monitoring tended to stay at the same level or increase (Table A7.3(b) in Appendix 3). This is perhaps not surprising given that schools can still have occasional visits from the HMI, even after the removal of special measures. Another reason for maintaining the same level of monitoring may be that these schools, having been through special measures, are even more conscientious than other schools. One head who reported that LEA monitoring had decreased significantly, but that school self-monitoring remained the same, explained that, 'As a school we are determined not to need special measures again, therefore [we] continue to work and monitor'.

As Tables A7.3(a) and A7.3(b) illustrate, a (comparatively) small number of respondents reported negative trends in the school following the removal of special measures, that is an increase in illness, stress, hours worked and a fall in job security and satisfaction. Their comments suggest that some of these schools were experiencing what could be called 'post-special measures blues' – once they had achieved their goal, they seemed to lose direction and motivation, or the removal from the register was not as liberating as they had expected. One teacher at a school recently removed from special measures pointed out:

[There was] *much staff illness. Loss of sense of purpose, increased job insecurity since decisions are less 'urgent'. Very little consistency in anything. Job descriptions still vague, not clear visions of how and when.* (Teacher)

Expected to be less stressed. Staff continue to be/feel under pressure. (Head)

One of the teachers who reported that job security had decreased substantially explained that 'money spent on new resources has resulted in financial deficits and therefore job losses'. He went on to say that 'we have spent a fortune to satisfy OFSTED and "improve standards"'.

Respondents were asked if any other aspects of their working lives had changed following the removal of special measures. The response rate to this open-ended question was low, with only about one-half of the headteachers and teachers answering, possibly because most of the changes had already been reported in the previous question. The main point made by one-fifth of heads and nearly one-fifth of teachers was that staff morale and self-confidence had improved. A sense that just as special measures had disempowered schools, once it had been removed, heads and staff felt that they were in charge again. One head refers to the 'psychological' changes at the school, particularly the 'feeling that we are now "masters of our own destiny"'. Similarly, another head said that 'we felt free to develop our own priorities at our own pace':

I now feel involved in 'real' school development rather than actions to get the school out of special measures. I also feel more confident and assured amongst colleagues. (Head)

The second most important point made by over 10 per cent of heads was that the amount of paperwork and bureaucracy had decreased. A further interesting point made by one headteacher was that once they had achieved their goal, team spirit and unity started to disintegrate:

Before removal – situation of head and staff united to face common threat from HMI; afterwards – as I maintained pressure for raising standards it became staff facing threat from me. (Head)

7.5 Effects of inspection and special measures

Chapter 6 described Survey 1 findings on the effects of inspection and action planning on the following aspects of school life:

- Quality of education provided.
- Educational standards achieved by pupils.
- Pupils' behaviour.
- Pupils' attendance levels.
- The working environment at the school.
- Teamwork amongst staff.
- Staff morale.
- Professional development opportunities.
- School's reputation in the community.
- Promotional opportunities for teachers.
- The school's ability to retain staff.
- The school's ability to recruit staff.

The same question was asked in Survey 2. The findings were broadly similar, though, not surprisingly, Survey 2 respondents were more likely to report that improvements had taken place. Quality of education and educational standards were the two areas which seemed to have improved the most. However, staff morale had deteriorated, according to nearly one-half of teachers and one-quarter of headteachers. See Tables A7.4(a) and A7.4(b) in Appendix 3.

Respondents to Survey 2 were also asked how confident they were that improvements made during special measures (if there were any) would be maintained once the school was removed from special measures. As Table 7.4 shows, the great majority of respondents were confident or very confident that the improvements would be maintained.

Table 7.4:   Maintaining improvements in the long term

	Heads	*Teachers*
	%	%
Level of confidence:		
Very confident	42	38
Confident	52	40
Not confident	1	9
Not at all confident	0	3
Unsure	1	7
No response	4	3
N	84	121

Because percentages are rounded to the nearest integer, they may not sum to 100 in all cases.

Heads and teachers were asked to comment on their answer. Most of the comments were from respondents who had expressed some degree of confidence that improvements would be maintained. They believed that improvements would be maintained because of:

• The mentality and outlook of staff. They had a positive attitude towards the future and were determined that improvements would be maintained.

• The recruitment and retention of high-quality staff.

• Strong leadership.

Some respondents who had indicated that the improvements would be maintained, acknowledged that this would be difficult.

Those heads and teachers who felt that improvements would **not** be maintained said that there had already been a reversal at their school, or that many of the changes had been short term or superficial. Others pointed out that improvement depended on retaining good staff, and this was not guaranteed. Interestingly, some of the interviewees suggested that working at a school which has been 'turned round' improves career prospects for staff. At one of the interview schools, the head (who had been appointed just before the inspection) and several teachers were leaving for better jobs elsewhere.

Respondents were also asked if they thought that 'the costs of inspection and action planning (in terms of time, effort, money, etc.) were worth the improvements which were made at the school'. As Table 7.5 shows, the percentage of teachers who said 'yes' or 'no' are very similar, though headteachers tended to be more positive.

Table 7.5: **Improvements and costs of inspection**

	Heads %	Teachers %
Improvements were worth costs		
Yes	60	43
No	30	39
Don't know	8	13
No response	2	5
N	84	121

Because percentages are rounded to the nearest integer, they may not sum to 100 in all cases.

Respondents were asked to comment on their answer. The main point made by those who had indicated that inspection had **not** been worth the cost was that money/resources would have been better spent on improving the school, or that the same result could have been achieved if schools had just been given the resources (nine heads and 13 teachers). In this respect, inspection was not cost-effective:

If the cost of the inspection had been devolved to the school budget, the improvements could have been achieved without the unnecessary stress and pressure that OFSTED brought. (Teacher)

The money involved could be better used on advisers, training, resources, including premises. (Teacher)

Other points raised by survey respondents included: headteachers appointed before inspection should be given a chance to implement their policies; improvements in the school would have occurred anyway due to new head or new government initiatives; and improvements could have been achieved with more support from the LEA. (Interview respondents made similar points regarding school improvement – see Chapter 6).

The main point made by those who felt that the costs **were** worth the outcome was that the school now had better policies and procedures and was generally in a much stronger position than it had been previously. Some of the other points included: the school was able to remove an ineffective head; there was greater accountability; and OFSTED speeded up/provided a focus for change. Some acknowledged that certain improvements had come at a price in terms of staff morale and well-being.

The final chapter of the report looks at the factors which helped schools come out of special measures and their insights/advice to schools which are currently on the special measures register.

Chapter 8

Coming Out of Special Measures

8.1 Factors which were significant in helping schools come out of special measures

Headteachers and teachers were asked to rate the importance of the following factors in helping their school to be removed from the special measures register:

- Receipt of additional resources

- Staff training

- Teamwork

- LEA inspection and advisory services

- School's self-monitoring system

- Teachers having more experience of inspection and monitoring

- Recruitment of a new headteacher (asked on the teachers' questionnaire only)

- Recruitment of new staff

- School management and leadership (teachers only)

- Liaison with other schools (headteachers only)

- Response from the governing body (headteachers only)

- Response from parents (headteachers only).

The results are shown in Tables A8.1(a) and A8.1(b), Appendix 3.[9] All of the factors listed above (with the exception of *Liaison with other schools*) were rated as important by the majority of respondents. For the teachers' sample, *School management and leadership* was the most frequently mentioned factor in helping schools come out of special measures, followed by *Teamwork*. The *School's self-monitoring system* and *Teamwork* were the two factors mentioned most often by headteachers.

---

[9] For details on the increased role of the LEA during special measures see Table A8.2 in Appendix 3.

Heads and teachers were also asked to list any other factors which had been instrumental in the school's removal from special measures. The two main factors were: the determination and hard work of staff, and the support/advice given by the HMI. Over one-fifth of teachers and one-quarter of heads mentioned the determination and hard work of staff. Unity in the face of adversity seems to sum up the situation at some of the schools surveyed, as the following comments suggest:

The sheer hard work and determination of all the staff. (Teacher)

Close-knit supportive staff pulling together. (Teacher)

Staff prepared to burn the midnight oil. (Head)

The perceived shame or injustice of special measures also seemed to make respondents even more determined and focused in their efforts:

Total commitment from the staff to remove stigma from the school. (Teacher)

The staff were devastated by the judgement, but continued to work harder than ever to pull the school out of special measures. None of the staff accepted the judgement as true but were determined to be part of the team who worked on the action plan. Parents, governors and LEA were also unable to accept the judgement and were very supportive of the school staff. (Head)

A willingness and a need for teachers to work to clear their name and [the] school, to get their professional status returned. (Teacher)

Support/advice from the HMI was mentioned by over one-quarter of headteachers, but fewer than 10 per cent of teachers. The HMI was seen as providing useful feedback and support, as the following examples show:

The HMI inspector was constructive throughout the process. On each monitoring visit he would tell us clearly where he thought we had made progress. Then he would set us some, what I thought, manageable targets for improvements before his next visit. Whilst it is a very traumatic process for all concerned – staff, students and all people associated with the school – it obviously did help us to improve. (Head)

He [HMI] *was my main source of help and praise, I had very little from my LEA. He was my lifeline.* (Head)

8.2 Advice to schools which are still on special measures

Heads and teachers were asked what insights or advice they would give to schools which were still on the special measures register. The following are the main points:

- Approximately four out of ten teachers and three out of ten heads mentioned the importance of mutual support and working together as a team. Some heads advised their counterparts in special measures schools to support their staff:

  To people at the helm I would advise gentle handling of fragile people who need encouragement and praise to keep them going in order to succeed. (Head)

  Back your staff, give them the skills, knowledge and confidence to exercise their duties and support them as much as possible. (Head)

- A related point raised by one-third of teachers and 27 per cent of heads is what could be called the psychology of coming off special measures. Schools were advised to think positively and not to give up hope. For example, one head pointed out: 'Aim to be positive for yourself, the staff and the school as a whole.' 'Do not give up', 'keep at it' and 'believe in yourselves' were typical of comments made by respondents. Schools were also reminded to focus on the ultimate reward for their hard work:

Remind yourself and your staff that you will feel a great sense of satisfaction when removed from special measures. (Head)

- Planning and target-setting was raised by one-third of headteachers and one-fifth of teachers. Respondents described the importance of thorough, focused plans which set ambitious but realistic goals for the school. Typical comments included: 'Be thorough in planning but always make sure tasks and timescale are achievable' (Head); and 'Set challenging targets and focus on achieving them' (Head).

- Effective monitoring was one of the main points raised by (one fifth) of headteachers. Interestingly, only one percent of teachers mentioned monitoring.

- Some of the other points (raised by between five and 15 per cent of heads and/or teachers) included: strong/good leadership from the headteacher and SMT; getting support from the LEA, governors and parents; listening to the advice of the HMI; accepting and coming to terms with failing the inspection; hard work; consulting staff and involving them in decision-making; effective record-keeping; and being willing to challenge the advice of HMI or OFSTED if necessary.

A few respondents recommended 'beating OFSTED at their own game', for example: 'Find out what OFSTED are looking for and show them what they want to see' (Teacher); and 'You have got to play along with the game to succeed!' (Teacher).

Chapter 9
Conclusions

This study set out to look at the effects of inspection and special measures on different aspects of school life. The project looked at teachers' and headteachers' perceptions of what it is like to work in a special measures school, and at how the process impacted upon workload, stress levels, job satisfaction and security. The link between the inspection process and school improvement was also explored. Drawing on the research, the following general conclusions can be made about the effects of inspection and special measures.

One of the overall findings of the research has been that headteachers are consistently more positive about inspection, compared with teaching staff. The fact that a far higher proportion of headteachers joined the school either immediately before or after the inspection may be significant in explaining their more positive outlook.

Schools were usually placed under special measures because of problems in one or more of the following areas: the quality of teaching; poor exam results/under-achievement; management issues; behaviour and attendance; and failure to implement the National Curriculum. Most headteachers at special measures and non-special measures schools felt that the key issues identified by the OFSTED team were appropriate and (to a lesser extent) expected. These findings are in line with previous research and may indicate that 'snapshot' inspections can give a reasonably accurate picture of a school and provide advice with which headteachers agree. On the other hand, it does raise questions as to whether inspections are simply identifying issues and problems which schools are already aware of (Centre for the Evaluation of Public Policy and Practice and Helix Consulting Group, 1999).

The period after inspection at special measures schools seems to be traumatic, as teachers and heads try to come to terms with feelings of shock, disappointment and disillusionment. Their initial reactions to the outcome of inspection included shock, a belief that the inspection was unfair or partial in some way, and feelings of depression and despondency ('post-OFSTED blues'). Respondents (particularly teachers) were concerned about the conduct of the inspection and the accuracy of the outcome. Perhaps not surprisingly, special measures schools were more likely to report that the outcome was too negative, compared with other schools. A recent OFSTED publication has recommended that teachers should try to come to terms with the inspection findings quickly and not 'indulge in retrospective apportioning of blame' (OFSTED, 1999). However, on the basis of this and other research studies, it seems that it is difficult for schools to accept special measures status when they have serious misgivings about the OFSTED system as a whole and/or the conduct of their own particular inspection (see also Ouston and Davies, 1998).

One of the most obvious differences between the special measures and non-special measures cohorts was the level of monitoring after inspection. Monitoring at special measures schools increased and became more systematic and thorough. Differences between the two groups were most evident in the case of LEA monitoring. Interestingly, the level of internal monitoring by the schools themselves seems to have increased for both samples, although this increase was far greater in the case of special measures schools. Previous research has suggested that a 'culture of inspection' has developed in schools generally and this may in part be attributed to the OFSTED system of inspection (Centre for the Evaluation of Public Policy and Practice and Helix Consulting Group, 1999).

Interview data suggested that the majority of respondents found the HMI inspections more useful and constructive than their OFSTED inspection. Although the preparation for HMI visits did add to workload and stress levels, respondents seemed to respect the advice they were given. The HMI tended to be seen as a 'critical friend'.

Survey and interview data suggested that the most difficult aspects of special measures were: the ongoing monitoring by HMI, the LEA and the school itself; a sense of deprofessionalisation and loss of confidence in their own ability; labelling and the 'naming and shaming' of failing schools; and increased workload, particularly in terms of planning and paperwork. It seems ironic that whilst the government is committed to reducing the 'bureaucratic burden' in schools, those schools which are seen as particularly weak and in need of special measures appear to have the highest level of paperwork. In some cases, the stress and workload had affected respondents' health or their private lives.

One of the more positive outcomes of the special measures process was that it seemed to unite staff in the pursuit of a common goal. Data from schools which are currently or have previously been on special measures suggested that mutual support helped teachers to cope during what was regarded as a very challenging period in their working lives. When asked about the factors which were significant in helping schools come out of special measures, 'management and leadership' and 'teamwork' were mentioned most frequently by teachers. The role of the LEA increased substantially in schools which were placed under special measures. The governing body also became more involved, though headteachers seemed more aware and more appreciative of their role than did teachers.

In terms of school improvement, the data indicate that the inspection process had a more profound effect on special measures schools than on other schools. The quality of education and, to a lesser extent, standards achieved by pupils were the two areas which seemed to have improved the most at special measures schools. Interview data suggested that these improvements were due to one or more of the following: changes in management; increased funding and advisory support; and the focus and urgency which the special measures process entails.

However, there were also some aspects of school life which seem to have deteriorated substantially since inspection, most notably staff morale. The contrast between declining staff morale and improvements in standards in education was one of the main findings of the research: there would appear to be an inverse relationship between the two variables. Whilst acknowledging that improvements had been made, most of those interviewed felt that there were better and more effective ways of achieving the same ends. They recognised that changes were necessary at their schools, but felt that the level of stress and 'public humiliation' generated by the process was unnecessary and even counter-productive. It was felt that whilst the special measures process had addressed some problems, it had also created new problems or aggravated existing ones.

Finally, the interview and survey data indicated that teachers were not opposed to school inspection as such, and believed that accountability in education was essential. They objected to the OFSTED model of inspection because it seemed to create as many problems as it solved.

Bibliography

ARIS, V., DAVIES, J. and JOHNSON, P. (1998). 'Brookfield special school: recovery from failure.' In: EARLEY, P. (Ed) *School Improvement after Inspection? School and LEA Responses.* London: Paul Chapman.

BOOTHROYD, C., FITZ-GIBBON, C., McNICHOLAS, J., THOMPSON, M., STERN, E. and WRAGG, T. (1997). *A Better System of Inspection?* Hexham: Office for Standards in Inspection.

BRIMBLECOMBE, N., ORMSTON, M. and SHAW, M. (1996a). 'Gender differences in teacher response to school inspection', *Educational Studies*, **22**, 1, 27-40.

BRIMBLECOMBE, N., ORMSTON, M. and SHAW, M. (1996b). 'Teachers' perceptions of inspections.' In: OUSTON, J., EARLEY, P. and FIDLER, B. (Eds) *OFSTED Inspections: the Early Experience.* London: David Fulton.

CENTRE FOR THE EVALUATION OF PUBLIC POLICY AND PRACTICE and HELIX CONSULTING GROUP (1999). *The OFSTED System of School Inspection: an Independent Evaluation.* Uxbridge: Centre for the Evaluation of Public Policy and Practice.

EARLEY, P. (1997). 'External inspections, "failing schools" and the role of governing bodies', *School Leadership & Management*, **17**, 3, 387-400.

EARLEY, P., FIDLER, B. and OUSTON, J. (Eds) (1998). *Improvement through Inspection? Complementary Approaches to School Development.* London: David Fulton.

FERGUSON, N., EARLEY, P., OUSTON, J. and FIDLER, B. (1999a). The Inspection of Primary Schools: Factors Associated with School Development. Unpublished report.

FERGUSON, N., EARLEY, P., OUSTON, J. and FIDLER, B. (1999b). 'New heads, OFSTED inspections and the prospects for school improvement', *Educational Research*, **41**, 3, 241-249.

FIDLER, B., EARLEY, P., OUSTON, J. and DAVIES, J. (1998). 'Teacher gradings and OFSTED inspections: help or hindrance as a management tool?' *School Leadership & Management*, **18**, 2, 257-70.

FISHER, D. (1999). *Partnership for Progress: Support for Underachieving Schools*. Slough: NFER, EMIE.

GANN, N. (1998). *Improving School Governance: How Better Governors Make Better Schools*. London: Falmer Press.

GREAT BRITAIN. PARLIAMENT. HOUSE OF COMMONS. EDUCATION AND EMPLOYMENT COMMITTEE (1999a). *The Work of OFSTED. Volume 1: Report and Proceedings of the Committee* (Fourth Report). London: The Stationery Office.

GREAT BRITAIN. PARLIAMENT. HOUSE OF COMMONS. EDUCATION AND EMPLOYMENT COMMITTEE (1999b). *Government's and OFSTED's Response to the Fourth Report from the Committee, Session 1998-99: the Work of OFSTED* (Fifth Special Report). London: The Stationery Office.

HOSKER, H. and ROBB, S. (1998). 'Raising standards and raising morale: a case study of change.' In: EARLEY, P. (Ed) *School Improvement after Inspection? School and LEA Responses*. London: Paul Chapman.

JEFFREY, B. and WOODS, P. (1996). 'Feeling deprofessionalised: the social construction of emotions during an OFSTED inspection', *Cambridge Journal of Education*, **26**, 3, 325-43.

JEFFREY, B. and WOODS, P. (1998). *Testing Teachers: the Effect of School Inspections on Primary Teachers*. London: Falmer Press.

MAYCHELL, K. and PATHAK, S. (1997). *Planning for Action Part 1: a Survey of Schools' Post-inspection Action Planning.* Slough: NFER.

OFFICE FOR STANDARDS IN EDUCATION (1998). *Making the Most of Inspection: a Guide to Inspection for Schools and Governors* (The Ofsted Handbook). London: OFSTED.

OFFICE FOR STANDARDS IN EDUCATION (1999). *Lessons Learned from Special Measures.* London: OFSTED.

OUSTON, J. and DAVIES, J. (1998). 'OFSTED and afterwards? Schools' responses to inspection.' In: EARLEY, P. (Ed) *School Improvement after Inspection? School and LEA Responses.* London: Paul Chapman.

OUSTON, J., FIDLER, B., EARLEY, P. and DAVIES, J. (1998). Making the Most of Inspection? The Impact of OFSTED Inspection on Secondary Schools. Unpublished report.

OUSTON, J. and KLENOWSKI, V. (1995). *The OFSTED Experience: the Parents' Eye View. Some Parents' Experience of OFSTED Secondary School Inspections.* London: Research and Information on State Education Trust.

PAGE, B. and AMES, A. (1998). *School Inspection Survey: Views of Primary Schools in England Inspected in Summer 1998.* London: MORI.

RILEY, K. and ROWLES, D. (1997). *Learning from Failure.* London: Haringey Council Education Services, School Effectiveness Branch.

TABBERER, R. (1995). *Parents' Perceptions of OFSTED's Work.* Slough: NFER.

THOMAS, G. (1996). 'The new schools' inspection system: some problems and possible solutions', *Educational Management & Administration,* **24**, 4, 355-69.

WILCOX, B. and GRAY, J. (1996). *Inspecting Schools: Holding Schools to Account and Helping Schools to Improve.* Buckingham: Open University Press.

Key issues and monitoring

- The majority of schools were placed under special measures for one or more of the following reasons: the quality of teaching was unsatisfactory; poor exam results/underachievement; lack of leadership/management problems; behaviour and attendance problems; and failure to implement the National Curriculum.

- The three main key issues for action at special measures schools were: the need to improve levels of attainment/exam results; the need to improve the quality of teaching; and the need to address management problems. Improving attainment, implementing the National Curriculum and increasing the amount of assessment were the most frequently mentioned key issues at non-special measures schools.

- The vast majority of headteachers said that most or all of the key issues identified by the inspection team were appropriate. The data suggest that headteachers at non-special measures schools were more likely to have anticipated the key issues for action.

- Interview data suggested that the majority of respondents found the HMI inspections more useful and constructive than their OFSTED inspection. Although the preparation for HMI visits did add to workload and stress levels, respondents seemed to respect the advice they were given.

- The majority of respondents (from special measures and non-special measures schools) indicated that the following types of monitoring were in use at their schools: observation of teaching; checking of documentation prepared by teachers, e.g. lesson plans, paperwork, and meetings/interviews regarding progress.

- Headteachers from special measures and non-special measures schools reported that staff monitoring had become more systematic and thorough since their last OFSTED inspection.

- The level of staff monitoring by the school itself seems to have increased substantially for both samples, although this increase was far greater in the case of special measures schools. Differences between the two samples were particularly evident in the case of LEA monitoring, where fewer than one-third of respondents at non-special measures schools reported an increase, compared with over three-quarters at special measures schools.

- Nearly one-half of the teachers and two-thirds of heads at non-special measures schools thought that the current level of staff monitoring was correct. The proportions were reversed for special measures schools, where about two-thirds of teachers but less than 50 per cent of heads were satisfied with current levels.

Stress and workload

- The majority of respondents from both samples agreed that they were 'under uncomfortable pressure because of workload'. Teachers at special measures schools were the group most likely to experience pressure at work and concerns over job security.

- Heads and teachers at special measures schools were more likely to agree with the statement that they 'work longer hours each week than do teachers at other schools'. The majority attributed their longer working hours to one or more of the following: the amount of paperwork they have to complete; lesson preparation; the school's special measures status; and the number of meetings which they have to attend.

- The average number of hours worked by heads at special measures schools was 63, whilst that for heads at non-special measures schools was 58. Teachers at special measures schools were working an average of 56 hours per week, compared with an average of 53 hours worked by teachers at other schools.

- A small proportion of teachers and heads from both samples reported taking time off due to illness before their OFSTED inspection. During the post-inspection period, the figures for time off due to illness increased for both samples, though the figures are noticeably higher for teachers at special measures schools.

- Interviewees reported that the most difficult aspects of working in a special measures school were: the level of monitoring; the labelling of the school as a 'failing' school; deprofessionalisation and loss of self-confidence amongst staff; and increased workload and changing nature of their work (that is, more paperwork and meetings).

Professional support and relationships

- The current research found that the LEAs supported special measures schools, mainly through increased funding/resources and advisory services. The majority of respondents felt that the LEA had been helpful and that relations between the school and the LEA had improved after the inspection. However, some were critical of the fact that their LEA had waited until after the school had failed its inspection before providing this level of support. It was felt that if LEAs had intervened sooner, then schools might not have been put on special measures.

- The findings suggest that although headteachers found the governing body supportive after special measures had been imposed, the majority of teachers were either unsure about governing body input or found it to be neither helpful nor unhelpful.

- One of the most important sources of support appeared to come from within the school itself. Staff united in the face of adversity and provided mutual support. In most cases, relations between staff themselves, and between staff and management, appeared to have improved following the inspection.

School improvement, staff changes and staff morale

- Not surprisingly, the inspection process seemed to have had a more profound effect on special measures schools, compared with other schools.

- The two areas which improved most during special measures were 'quality of education' and, to a lesser extent, 'standards achieved by pupils'.

- There were also some aspects of school life which seemed to have deteriorated substantially since inspection. This was most notable in relation to staff morale, as reported by teachers from both groups of schools. These findings are in line with previous research which suggests that schools generally can experience 'post-OFSTED blues' in the year after inspection (Ferguson *et al.*, 1999).

- Interviewees at special measures schools attributed improvements in the quality of education and educational standards to one or more of the following factors: changes in management; increased funding and advisory support; and the sense of focus and urgency which the special measures process brings.

- Whilst acknowledging that improvements had been made, most of those interviewed felt that there were better and more cost-effective ways of achieving the same ends. It was felt that whilst the process had addressed some problems, it had also created new problems or aggravated existing ones. For example, in cases where the allocation of additional resources or the employment of additional staff was the key factor in improving standards, teachers asked why this could not have been done earlier.

- The current study found that there was far more stability, in terms of staffing, at non-special measures schools. Differences between the two groups were most evident for resignations, retirements on grounds of ill-health and competency/disciplinary procedures in the year after the inspection.

- Only about half of the headteachers at special measures schools had worked at their current school (either as head or in another role) during the last OFSTED inspection. About one-fifth of teachers at special measures schools had not been employed at their current school during the last inspection.

- Interviewees were in favour of accountability in education but objected to the OFSTED system of inspection because it appeared to create as many problems as it solved. They were in favour of a system which would provide more than a 'snapshot' view and which would have an advisory/supportive function. It was felt that the current OFSTED system of inspection provides surveillance without support.

Experience of former special measures schools

- Like their Survey 1 counterparts, schools no longer on special measures reported that their initial reactions to failing their inspection were: shock; a belief that the inspection was unfair or partial in some way; and feelings of disappointment and despondency.

- There were some areas where substantial improvements had been made to teachers' lives following the removal of special measures. For example, respondents reported a reduction in stress levels and greater job security. In other areas there had been little change (e.g. levels of internal monitoring by the school) and in a small number of cases, there had been a deterioration of some aspect of school life.

- The majority of respondents reported that they were confident that the improvements made during special measures would be maintained. They explained their answer by saying that their school had recruited high-quality teachers and that staff had a positive outlook towards the future. Those who felt that improvements would not be maintained said that there had already been a reversal at their school, or that many of the changes had been short term or superficial. Others pointed out that improvement depended on retaining good staff, and this was not guaranteed.

- Respondents were also asked if they thought that 'the costs of inspection and action planning (in terms of time, effort, money, etc.) were worth the improvements which were made at the school'. The percentage of teachers who said 'yes' or 'no' are very similar (about 40 per cent respectively), though headteachers were more positive.

- Those who indicated that inspection had not been worth the cost said that the money and other resources would have been better spent on improving the school, or that the same result could have been achieved if schools had just been given the resources. The main point made by those who felt that the costs were worth the outcome was that the school now had better policies and procedures and was generally in a much stronger position than it had been previously.

- When asked what advice or insights they would offer to schools which were still on the special measures register, respondents emphasised the importance of: mutual support and working as a team; thorough, focused plans which set ambitious but realistic goals for the school; effective monitoring (headteachers); and determination and a positive approach.

Appendix 1:
Background information on respondents and schools

Background information on Survey 1 respondents

Table A1.1: Gender of respondents

	Schools on special measures		Schools not on special measures	
	Heads %	Teachers %	Heads %	Teachers %
Male	40	25	40	21
Female	57	71	53	75
No response	3	4	7	5
N	173	294	255	442

Because percentages are rounded to the nearest integer, they may not sum to 100 in all cases.

Table A1.2: Headteachers' position

	Heads at special measures schools %	Heads at non-special measures schools %
Permanent headship post	80	94
Acting headteacher	19	5
No response	1	2
N	173	255

Because percentages are rounded to the nearest integer, they may not sum to 100 in all cases.

Table A1.3: Teachers' position in school

	Schools on special measures	Schools not on special measures
	Teachers %	Teachers %
Member of the SMT	40	31
Holder of a post of paid responsibility	57	54
Holder of a post of unpaid responsibility	40	36
Class teacher with no other formal responsibilities	10	13
No response	1	1
N	294	442

A multiple-response question: therefore percentages may not sum to 100.

Table A1.4: Number of years' experience/years at this school

	Schools on special measures		Schools not on special measures	
	Heads %	Teachers %	Heads %	Teachers %
Number of years at this school*				
Less than 1 year	8	0	4	0
1 year	38	18	11	7
2 – 5 years	42	30	34	30
6 – 10 years	8	25	27	27
Over 10 years	4	26	21	35
No response	2	1	4	2
Number of years of headship experience				
1 year or less	19	-	10	-
2 – 5 years	34	-	26	-
6 – 10 years	24	-	26	-
11 – 15 years	13	-	20	-
Over 15 years	6	-	11	-
No response	4	-	7	-
Total number of years in the teaching profession				
5 years or less	0	20	0	18
6 – 10 years	2	20	0	14
11 – 15 years	5	13	4	10
16 – 20 years	21	15	16	14
21 – 30 years	61	29	59	37
Over 30 years	8	2	17	5
No response	3	1	4	2
N	173	294	255	442

Because percentages are rounded to the nearest integer, they may not sum to 100 in all cases.
* For headteachers, as head or acting head of the school.

Table A1.5: Curriculum area of teachers

	Schools on special measures Teachers %		Schools not on special measures Teachers %
Curriculum area:		**Curriculum area:**	
Science	12	Science	16
English	10	Modern Languages	10
Technology	10	Mathematics	9
Mathematics	9	English	8
PE	9	History	7
Modern Languages	8	Technology	7
Art	5	PE	5
Religious Education	5	Geography	3
SEN	3	Music	3
Humanities	3	Art	2
History	3	Religious Education	2
IT	2	SEN	2
Music	2	Accountancy	2
PSE	2	Home Economics	2
Geography	1	Humanities	1
Home Economics	1	PSE	1
Not applicable	0	Not applicable	1
No response	17	No response	20
N*	116	**N***	173

Because percentages are rounded to the nearest integer, they may not sum to 100 in all cases.
* Primary school teachers were not asked to name their main curriculum area, therefore the sample numbers in the above table are smaller than that in the other tables.

Table A1.6: Date of last inspection

	Schools on special measures		Schools not on special measures	
	Heads %	Teachers %	Heads %	Teachers %
1993 – 1995	7	7	5	7
1996	15	16	24	20
1997	42	37	24	26
1998	37	40	37	39
1999	0	0	10	9
N	173	294	255	442

Because percentages are rounded to the nearest integer, they may not sum to 100 in all cases.

Table A1.7: School phase

	Schools on special measures				Schools not on special measures			
	Heads		Teachers		Heads		Teachers	
	N*	%	N	%	N	%	N	%
Primary	122	71	178	61	170	67	269	61
Secondary	24	14	72	25	41	16	118	27
Special	26	15	43	15	42	17	51	12
No response	1	1	1	0	2	1	4	1
Total	173	100	294	100	255	100	442	100

Because percentages are rounded to the nearest integer, they may not sum to 100 in all cases.
*N is the number of schools.

Table A1.8: Catchment area

Catchment area	Schools on special measures Heads	Schools not on special measures Heads
	%	%
Country town/rural	22	21
Suburban	9	16
Inner city/urban	65	59
No response	4	4
N	173	255

Because percentages are rounded to the nearest integer, they may not sum to 100 in all cases.

Background information on Survey 2 respondents

Table A1.9: Gender of respondents

	Heads %	Teachers %
Male	35	13
Female	65	84
No response	0	3
N	84	121

Because percentages are rounded to the nearest integer, they may not sum to 100 in all cases.

Table A1.10: Headteachers' position

	Heads %
Permanent headship post	91
Acting headteacher	10
N	84

Because percentages are rounded to the nearest integer, they may not sum to 100 in all cases.

Table A1.11: Teachers' position in school

	Teachers %
Member of the SMT	27
Holder of a post of paid responsibility	42
Holder of a post of unpaid responsibility	27
Class teacher with no other formal responsibilities	3
No response	1
N	121

A multiple-response question: therefore percentages may not sum to 100.

Table A1.12: Number of years' experience/years at this school

	Heads %	Teachers %
Number of years at this school*		
Less than 1 year	4	0
1 year	12	8
2 – 5 years	76	32
6 – 10 years	6	25
Over 10 years	1	34
No response	1	1
Number of years of headship experience		
1 year or less	10	-
2 – 5 years	54	-
6 – 10 years	25	-
11 – 15 years	4	-
Over 15 years	2	-
No response	6	-
Total number of years in the teaching profession		
5 years or less	0	18
6 – 10 years	5	12
11 – 15 years	6	10
16 – 20 years	18	21
21 – 30 years	66	36
Over 30 years	4	2
No response	2	2
N	84	121

Because percentages are rounded to the nearest integer, they may not sum to 100 in all cases.
* For headteachers, as head of the school.

Table A1.13: Working in school at time of inspection

	Heads %	Teachers %
Yes, as headteacher	39	-
Yes	14	74
No	45	25
No response	1	1
N	84	121

Because percentages are rounded to the nearest integer, they may not sum to 100 in all cases.

Table A1.14: Catchment area

Catchment area	Heads
	%
Country town/rural	27
Suburban	10
Inner city/urban	63
No response	0
N	84

Because percentages are rounded to the nearest integer, they may not sum to 100 in all cases.

Table A1.15: School type

	Heads		Teachers	
	N	%	N	%
Primary	63	75	76	63
Secondary	11	13	26	22
Special	10	12	19	16
Total	84	100	121	100

Because percentages are rounded to the nearest integer, they may not sum to 100 in all cases.

Date of inspection

Not surprisingly, respondents to Survey 2 had their inspection earlier than those involved in Survey 1. The majority of schools responding to Survey 1 were inspected in 1997 or 1998, whereas most of those in Survey 2 were inspected between 1996 and 1997.

Table A1.16: Date of last inspection

Date	Heads	Teachers
	%	%
1993 – 1995	32	36
1996	41	38
1997	26	25
1998	1	2
N	84	121

Because percentages are rounded to the nearest integer, they may not sum to 100 in all cases.

Table A1.17: Date of removal from special measures

Date	Heads	Teachers
	%	%
1995	2	2
1996	-	1
1997	20	16
1998	66	62
1999	8	13
No response	4	7
N	84	121

Because percentages are rounded to the nearest integer,
they may not sum to 100 in all cases.

Appendix 2:
Tables for Chapters 2 – 6
(Survey 1 data)

Table A3.1: Number of times teaching has been monitored

	Schools on special measures	Schools not on special measures
	Teachers	*Teachers*
Monitored by:	%	%
Headteacher or member of SMT		
Never	12	27
Three times or less	55	55
Four times or more	30	12
No response	4	7
A middle manager		
Never	29	34
Three times or less	41	39
Four times or more	10	5
No response	20	22
Other teaching staff		
Never	41	45
Three times or less	27	24
Four times or more	5	5
No response	28	27
A school governor		
Never	38	48
Three times or less	35	23
Four times or more	7	3
No response	20	26
An LEA inspector/adviser		
Never	10	38
Three times or less	59	41
Four times or more	24	3
No response	7	17
An HMI inspector*		
Never	5	60
Three times or less	68	6
Four times or more	22	4
No response	4	31
N	294	442

Because percentages are rounded to the nearest integer, they may not sum to 100 in all cases.

*Schools which are not in the serious weakness or special measures categories do not normally have HMI visits, therefore the considerable difference in the results for the special measures and non-special measures groups is to be expected here.

Levels of monitoring in schools

On average, heads at special measures schools reported that they had monitored 30 lessons and 15 individual teachers during the current school year. Headteachers at non-special measures schools said that they had monitored 15 lessons and nine individual teachers during this time.

Headteachers were also asked about the frequency of LEA visits, the number of classes observed by LEA advisers/inspectors and the number of meetings between the head and these advisers/inspectors during the current school year. In each case, the average (mean) number was considerably higher for special measures schools. For example, the average number of LEA visits to special measures schools was 12, compared with only three for non-special measures schools. LEA advisers/inspectors observed an average of 22 lessons at special measures schools, compared with an average of six lessons at non-special measures schools.

Table A4.1: Workload and stress

	Schools on special measures		Schools not on special measures	
	Heads %	Teachers %	Heads %	Teachers %
Uncomfortable pressure due to workload				
Agree	71	83	77	71
Disagree	27	14	22	23
Not sure	1	2	2	3
No response	1	0	0	2
Deterioration in job performance due to stress				
Agree	27	51	46	45
Disagree	68	42	44	49
Not sure	4	5	9	5
No response	2	2	2	1
Concern about job security				
Agree	25	42	16	20
Disagree	64	51	81	72
Not sure	5	6	2	7
No response	6	1	2	1
I work longer hours				
Agree	69	67	28	33
Disagree	16	19	49	45
Not sure	13	14	21	21
No response	1	0	2	1
N	173	294	255	442

Because percentages are rounded to the nearest integer, they may not sum to 100 in all cases.

Table A5.1: Professional support for teachers

		Schools on special measures	Schools not on special measures
		Teachers %	*Teachers* %
Headteacher			
	Helpful	57	60
	Neither helpful nor unhelpful	20	25
	Unhelpful	16	8
	Unable to say	5	4
	No response	2	4
Other SMT			
	Helpful	58	58
	Neither helpful nor unhelpful	20	26
	Unhelpful	9	4
	Unable to say	9	4
	No response	5	8
Middle managers			
	Helpful	56	62
	Neither helpful nor unhelpful	22	22
	Unhelpful	4	2
	Unable to say	10	5
	No response	8	9
Other teachers			
	Helpful	69	71
	Neither helpful nor unhelpful	19	20
	Unhelpful	3	1
	Unable to say	5	3
	No response	3	6
Governors			
	Helpful	22	18
	Neither helpful nor unhelpful	49	55
	Unhelpful	17	13
	Unable to say	9	10
	No response	3	4
LEA advisers/inspectors			
	Helpful	48	31
	Neither helpful nor unhelpful	22	42
	Unhelpful	20	12
	Unable to say	8	11
	No response	2	4
Other			
	Helpful	15	6
	Neither helpful nor unhelpful	2	3
	Unhelpful	2	0
	Unable to say	5	3
	No response	76	88
	N	294	442

Because percentages are rounded to the nearest integer, they may not sum to 100 in all cases.

Table A5.2(a): Changes in professional relationships

	Schools on special measures		Schools not on special measures	
	Heads %	*Teachers* %	*Heads* %	*Teachers* %
Between SMT and other teaching staff				
Improved	54	44	17	14
No change	17	26	66	65
Deteriorated	8	16	7	12
Unable to say	7	10	5	6
No response	15	4	6	3
Within the SMT				
Improved	58	-	29	-
No change	15	-	54	-
Deteriorated	5	-	7	-
Unable to say	7	-	4	-
No response	15	-	6	-
Between the head and teaching staff				
Improved	55	44	19	17
No change	19	16	60	55
Deteriorated	5	21	11	19
Unable to say	9	13	4	6
No response	13	5	6	4
Amongst teaching staff				
Improved	55	40	20	22
No change	20	38	61	60
Deteriorated	6	13	12	12
Unable to say	6	7	4	4
No response	12	3	4	2
Between the head and governors				
Improved	59	-	29	-
No change	16	-	60	-
Deteriorated	2	-	4	-
Unable to say	9	-	4	-
No response	14	-	4	-
N	173	294	255	442

Because percentages are rounded to the nearest integer, they may not sum to 100 in all cases.

Table A5.2(b): Changes in professional relationships

	Schools on special measures		Schools not on special measures	
	Heads %	*Teachers* %	*Heads* %	*Teachers* %
Between teaching staff and governors				
Improved	46	36	18	12
No change	27	37	67	64
Deteriorated	5	6	6	6
Unable to say	9	18	4	15
No response	13	3	5	3
Between teaching staff and pupils				
Improved	51	36	13	10
No change	27	43	74	76
Deteriorated	4	9	6	7
Unable to say	6	9	3	5
No response	12	3	4	2
Between teaching staff and parents				
Improved	43	31	17	14
No change	32	49	71	73
Deteriorated	6	7	5	4
Unable to say	6	11	3	6
No response	12	3	4	2
Between the school and LEA				
Improved	57	45	20	10
No change	16	20	60	58
Deteriorated	9	11	11	7
Unable to say	6	20	4	21
No response	13	4	4	3
N	173	294	255	442

Because percentages are rounded to the nearest integer, they may not sum to 100 in all cases.

Table A6.1(a): Effects of the inspection process

	Schools on special measures		Schools not on special measures	
	Heads	Teachers	Heads	Teachers
	%	%	%	%
Quality of education provided				
Improved	89	78	52	37
No change	5	14	39	53
Deteriorated	1	3	4	4
Unable to say	2	3	3	3
No response	3	1	3	4
Educational standards achieved by pupils				
Improved	79	60	33	26
No change	13	27	57	63
Deteriorated	2	3	4	3
Unable to say	4	9	3	5
No response	3	2	3	3
Pupils' behaviour				
Improved	59	41	9	7
No change	32	41	77	76
Deteriorated	6	14	8	12
Unable to say	2	2	3	2
No response	2	2	3	3
Pupils' attendance levels				
Improved	39	34	13	14
No change	53	55	77	73
Deteriorated	2	3	4	6
Unable to say	2	7	3	5
No response	4	2	4	2
Professional development opportunities				
Improved	72	43	28	18
No change	23	36	61	62
Deteriorated	1	14	4	14
Unable to say	2	5	4	3
No response	2	2	3	3
Promotional opportunities for teachers				
Improved	28	15	12	7
No change	49	41	75	71
Deteriorated	14	28	6	11
Unable to say	6	14	4	8
No response	4	3	3	3
The working environment at the school				
Improved	71	51	29	19
No change	17	21	55	54
Deteriorated	8	23	10	20
Unable to say	1	3	3	3
No response	3	2	3	3
N	173	294	255	442

Because percentages are rounded to the nearest integer, they may not sum to 100 in all cases.

In the questionnaire a six-point scale was used, ranging from 'Improved a lot' to 'Deteriorated a lot'. The data for 'Improved' and 'Improved a lot' were combined to form one category. Similarly, the data for 'Deteriorated' and 'Deteriorated a lot' were combined.

Table A6.1(b): Effects of the inspection process

		Schools on special measures		Schools not on special measures	
		Heads %	Teachers %	Heads %	Teachers %
Teamwork amongst staff					
	Improved	76	49	31	25
	No change	18	29	54	56
	Deteriorated	2	15	10	14
	Unable to say	2	5	2	3
	No response	2	2	3	3
Staff morale					
	Improved	50	25	17	11
	No change	11	9	40	36
	Deteriorated	32	58	36	48
	Unable to say	2	5	3	3
	No response	5	4	4	3
School's reputation in the community					
	Improved	41	30	35	28
	No change	24	25	51	51
	Deteriorated	26	35	7	10
	Unable to say	6	9	4	7
	No response	3	2	3	4
Schools' ability to recruit staff					
	Improved	17	-	9	-
	No change	36	-	73	-
	Deteriorated	36	-	9	-
	Unable to say	8	-	5	-
	No response	3	-	4	-
Schools' ability to retain staff					
	Improved	21	-	5	
	No change	46	-	80	
	Deteriorated	24	-	7	
	Unable to say	7	-	4	
	No response	3	-	4	
	N	173	294	255	442

Because percentages are rounded to the nearest integer, they may not sum to 100 in all cases.

Table A6.2(a): Changes to staffing figures after the inspection

Number of:	Schools on special measures Heads %	Schools not on special measures Heads %
Teaching staff		
Increased	22	14
Stayed the same	44	56
Decreased	27	21
Not applicable	0	0
Don't know	3	2
No response	4	7
New appointments		
Increased	63	35
Stayed the same	17	37
Decreased	4	4
Not applicable	7	15
Don't know	4	1
No response	4	7
Average number of applicants		
Increased	11	8
Stayed the same	25	44
Decreased	29	12
Not applicable	14	18
Don't know	16	7
No response	6	11
Resignations		
Increased	45	20
Stayed the same	21	39
Decreased	4	4
Not applicable	17	23
Don't know	6	4
No response	7	10
Retirements on grounds of ill-health		
Increased	34	12
Stayed the same	16	30
Decreased	3	3
Not applicable	33	42
Don't know	7	4
No response	8	10
Other retirements		
Increased	26	15
Stayed the same	22	29
Decreased	4	3
Not applicable	33	37
Don't know	8	4
No response	9	13
***N**	161	242

Because percentages are rounded to the nearest integer, they may not sum to 100 in all cases.

*The sample number is lower in the above table, as this question was only addressed to headteachers who had their school inspection from January 1996 onwards.

Table A6.2(b): Changes to staffing figures

	Schools on special measures	Schools not on special measures
	Heads %	Heads %
Redundancies		
Increased	17	8
Stayed the same	17	27
Decreased	2	2
Not applicable	45	46
Don't know	5	3
No response	14	14
Competency/disciplinary procedures		
Increased	51	17
Stayed the same	6	24
Decreased	3	2
Not applicable	29	47
Don't know	4	2
No response	7	10
Dismissals		
Increased	11	3
Stayed the same	16	24
Decreased	1	2
Not applicable	54	57
Don't know	6	2
No response	13	12
Staff sick leave		
Increased	54	38
Stayed the same	21	40
Decreased	12	5
Not applicable	3	5
Don't know	6	3
No response	6	9
N	161	242

Because percentages are rounded to the nearest integer, they may not sum to 100 in all cases.

*The sample number is lower in the above table, as this question was only addressed to headteachers who had their school inspection from January 1996 onwards.

Pupil Exclusions

Pupil numbers and exclusions may undergo change following an OFSTED inspection. Headteachers were asked if the number of exclusions had changed since the year before the last full OFSTED inspection. The results are shown in Table A6.3 below. The figures suggest that numbers of exclusions are more likely to undergo change at special measures schools.

Table A6.3: Numbers of exclusions

	Schools on special measures	Schools not on special measures
	Heads %	Heads %
Exclusions (fixed term)		
Increased	26	13
Stayed the same	19	42
Decreased	29	14
Not applicable	16	26
Don't know	3	1
No response	8	4
Exclusions (permanent)		
Increased	13	11
Stayed the same	25	35
Decreased	21	11
Not applicable	28	39
Don't know	4	1
No response	9	4
N	173	255

Because percentages are rounded to the nearest integer, they may not sum to 100 in all cases.

Additional resources/changes necessary for schools to be removed from special measures

The main points made by respondents were:

- The need for additional staff. (This point was made by approximately one-fifth of teachers and one-third of heads.)

- The need for additional resources (for example, computers) and funding. (About one-quarter of teachers and one-fifth of heads.)

- The need for stability at the senior management level was mentioned by about 10 per cent of heads and teachers. On the other hand, nearly 15 per cent of teachers said their school needed a new headteacher.

Appendix 3:
Tables for Chapters 7 and 8
(Survey 2)

Table A7.1: Key issues for action

	Heads %
Appropriateness of key issues:	
All were appropriate	51
Most were appropriate	29
Fewer than half were appropriate	7
A few were appropriate	7
None were appropriate	1
Don't know	1
No response	4
Expected key issues:	
All were expected	14
Most were expected	29
Fewer than half were expected	17
A few were expected	13
None were expected	5
Don't know	6
No response	17
N	84

Because percentages are rounded to the nearest integer,
they may not sum to 100 in all cases.

Table A7.2: Workload and stress

	Heads %	Teachers %
Uncomfortable pressure due to workload		
Agree	69	75
Disagree	25	22
Not sure	2	1
No response	4	2
Deterioration in job performance due to stress		
Agree	31	33
Disagree	64	58
Not sure	2	7
No response	2	3
Concern about job security		
Agree	17	22
Disagree	70	69
Not sure	8	5
No response	5	3
I work longer hours		
Agree	42	49
Disagree	37	29
Not sure	17	21
No response	5	2
N	84	121

Because percentages are rounded to the nearest integer, they may not sum to 100 in all cases.

Table A7.3(a) : Changes following the removal of special measures

	Heads %	Teachers %
Average hours worked		
Significant increase	11	12
Slight increase	7	8
No change	52	59
Slight decrease	23	14
Significant decrease	0	3
Not sure	1	0
No response	6	4
Level of stress		
Significant increase	12	10
Slight increase	11	15
No change	33	12
Slight decrease	21	26
Significant decrease	17	31
No response	6	7
Average number of days off due to illness		
Significant increase	1	2
Slight increase	1	10
No change	88	74
Slight decrease	1	4
Significant decrease	1	3
Not sure	1	2
No response	6	7
Level of job satisfaction		
Significant increase	19	24
Slight increase	23	25
No change	38	29
Slight decrease	10	11
Significant decrease	2	7
Not sure	1	0
No response	7	5
Number of applications for teaching posts		
Significant increase	6	–
Slight increase	17	–
No change	58	–
Slight decrease	2	–
Significant decrease	1	–
Not sure	4	–
No response	12	–
Confidence in job security		
Significant increase	12	16
Slight increase	16	18
No change	56	48
Slight decrease	4	8
Significant decrease	5	4
Not sure	2	1
No response	6	5
N	84	121

Because percentages are rounded to the nearest integer, they may not sum to 100 in all cases.
Not all questions were common to both heads and teachers, hence some of the cells in the above table are blank.

Table A7.3(b) : Changes following the removal of special measures

	Heads %	Teachers %
Amount of LEA monitoring		
Significant increase	5	7
Slight increase	5	10
No change	21	12
Slight decrease	27	26
Significant decrease	35	36
Not sure	0	3
No response	7	6
Amount of school self-monitoring		
Significant increase	17	21
Slight increase	17	18
No change	48	41
Slight decrease	13	14
Significant decrease	1	1
Not sure	0	1
No response	5	4
Governing body involvement		
Significant increase	11	–
Slight increase	17	–
No change	46	–
Slight decrease	16	–
Significant decrease	5	–
No response	6	–
Parental involvement		
Significant increase	5	–
Slight increase	11	–
No change	76	–
Slight decrease	2	–
Significant decrease	1	–
No response	5	–
Amount of financial support		
Significant increase	5	–
Slight increase	5	–
No change	35	–
Slight decrease	25	–
Significant decrease	24	–
No response	7	–
Number of pupil applications		
Significant increase	12	–
Slight increase	24	–
No change	50	–
Slight decrease	2	–
Significant decrease	4	–
Not sure	2	–
No response	6	–
N	84	121

Because percentages are rounded to the nearest integer, they may not sum to 100 in all cases.
Not all questions were common to both heads and teachers, hence some of the cells in the above table are blank.

Table A7.4(a): Effects of the inspection process

	Heads %	Teachers %
Quality of education provided		
Improved	95	90
No change	5	6
Deteriorated	0	1
Unable to say	0	2
No response	0	2
Educational standards achieved by pupils		
Improved	87	76
No change	12	19
Deteriorated	0	0
Unable to say	1	3
No response	0	2
Pupils' behaviour		
Improved	55	37
No change	45	50
Deteriorated	0	10
Unable to say	0	1
No response	0	2
Pupils' attendance levels		
Improved	31	35
No change	64	55
Deteriorated	2	2
Unable to say	0	6
No response	2	3
Professional development opportunities		
Improved	73	45
No change	23	36
Deteriorated	2	13
Unable to say	2	4
No response	0	3
Promotional opportunities for teachers		
Improved	36	22
No change	54	49
Deteriorated	5	15
Unable to say	5	10
No response	1	4
The working environment at the school		
Improved	73	68
No change	21	14
Deteriorated	1	14
Unable to say	2	2
No response	2	3
N	84	121

Because percentages are rounded to the nearest integer, they may not sum to 100 in all cases.

Table A7.4(b): Effects of the inspection process

		Heads %	Teachers %
Teamwork amongst staff			
	Improved	80	59
	No change	16	25
	Deteriorated	2	9
	Unable to say	1	5
	No response	1	3
Staff morale			
	Improved	63	35
	No change	8	13
	Deteriorated	24	47
	Unable to say	1	3
	No response	4	2
School's reputation in the community			
	Improved	73	49
	No change	13	23
	Deteriorated	8	19
	Unable to say	4	6
	No response	2	3
The school's ability to retain staff			
	Improved	37	–
	No change	46	–
	Deteriorated	10	–
	Unable to say	4	–
	No response	4	–
The school's ability to recruit staff			
	Improved	35	–
	No change	48	–
	Deteriorated	11	–
	Unable to say	5	–
	No response	2	–
N		84	121

Because percentages are rounded to the nearest integer, they may not sum to 100 in all cases.

Table A8.1(a): Factors which helped the school

		Heads %	Teachers %
Receipt of additional resources			
	Important	63	61
	Minor importance	13	18
	No importance	6	3
	Don't know	1	3
	Not applicable	10	5
	No response	7	10
Staff training			
	Important	82	69
	Minor importance	12	18
	No importance	1	3
	Don't know	0	1
	Not applicable	0	2
	No response	5	8
Teamwork			
	Important	93	98
	Minor importance	2	4
	No importance	0	0
	Don't know	1	1
	Not applicable	0	0
	No response	4	3
*Recruitment of new headteacher			
	Important	–	55
	Minor importance	–	2
	No importance	–	3
	Don't know	–	1
	*Not applicable	–	31
	No response	–	8
Recruitment of new staff			
	Important	73	58
	Minor importance	5	18
	No importance	11	6
	Don't know	1	0
	Not applicable	6	14
	No response	5	4
School management and leadership			
	Important	–	87
	Minor importance	–	7
	No importance	–	0
	Don't know	–	2
	Not applicable	–	0
	No response	–	5
N		84	121

Because percentages are rounded to the nearest integer, they may not sum to 100 in all cases.
Not all questions were common to both heads and teachers, hence some of the cells in the above table are blank.
*It should be noted that not all schools appointed a new headteacher.

Table A8.1(b): Factors which helped the school

		Heads %	Teachers %
LEA inspection and advisory services			
	Important	66	59
	Minor importance	19	30
	No importance	4	4
	Don't know	0	0
	Not applicable	2	0
	No response	7	7
School's self-monitoring system			
	Important	93	78
	Minor importance	4	12
	No importance	0	2
	Don't know	0	2
	Not applicable	0	1
	No response	4	7
Having more experience of monitoring and inspection			
	Important	61	65
	Minor importance	23	22
	No importance	7	5
	Don't know	2	1
	Not applicable	1	1
	No response	6	7
Liaison with other schools			
	Important	17	–
	Minor importance	44	–
	No importance	30	–
	Don't know	2	–
	Not applicable	2	–
	No response	5	–
Response from the governing body			
	Important	75	–
	Minor importance	12	–
	No importance	8	–
	Don't know	0	–
	Not applicable	1	–
	No response	4	–
Response from parents			
	Important	54	–
	Minor importance	25	–
	No importance	13	–
	Don't know	1	–
	Not applicable	0	–
	No response	7	–
N		84	121

Because percentages are rounded to the nearest integer, they may not sum to 100 in all cases. Not all questions were common to both heads and teachers, hence some of the cells in the above table are blank.

Table A8.2: LEA actions during special measures

	Heads %	Teachers %
Appointment of additional governors		
Yes	55	47
No	36	22
Don't know	0	17
Not applicable	2	3
No response	7	11
Allocation of additional resources		
Yes	77	78
No	17	7
Don't know	1	7
Not applicable	1	2
No response	4	6
Withdrawal of the delegated budget		
Yes	10	9
No	74	46
Don't know	0	27
Not applicable	5	3
No response	12	1
N	84	121

Because percentages are rounded to the nearest integer, they may not sum to 100 in all cases.

Appendix 4:
Response rates for open-ended questions
(Surveys 1 and 2)

Response rates for open-ended questions (Survey 1)

Reference in text:	Special measures schools		Non-special measures schools	
	Headteachers	Teachers	Headteachers	Teachers
Reactions to outcome of inspection (Chapter 2)	89%	95%	92%	95%
n*	85	234	230	424
Reasons for special measures (Chapter 3)	94%	91%	-	-
n	173	294		
Key Issues for Action (Chapter 3)	95%	-	93%	-
n	161	-	242	
Comments on changes in level of monitoring (Chapter 3)	84%	-	67%	-
n	173		255	
Reasons for longer working hours (Chapter 4)	95%	99%	96%	94%
n	120	198	71	147
Factors which discouraged staff (Chapter 4)	-	78%	-	61%
n		294		442
Factors which helped to support staff (Chapter 5)	-	67%	-	55%
n		294		442

*n is the number of respondents to whom a particular question was addressed. This may vary. For example, only those respondents who said that they worked longer hours than teachers in other schools were asked to comment on their answer. Similarly some questions were addressed to special measures schools only. The percentages column shows the percentage of respondents who actually answered the question.

Response rates for open-ended questions (Survey 2)

Reference in text:		Headteachers	Teachers
Other changes to working life (Chapter 7)		50%	60%
	n	84	121
Level of confidence in maintaining improvements (Chapter 7)		46%	45%
	n	84	121
Costs of inspection (Chapter 7)		57%	88%
	n	84	121
Factors which helped the school to come out of special measures (Chapter 8)		81%	59%
	n	84	121
Advice to schools currently on special measures (Chapter 8)		82%	82%
	n	84	121